Legend of the Blue Wings

Legend of the Blue Wings

Dawn Williscroft

iUniverse, Inc.
Bloomington

Legend of the Blue Wings

iUniverse books may be ordered through booksellers or by contacting:

iUniverse
1663 Liberty Drive
Bloomington, IN 47403
www.iuniverse.com
1-800-Authors (1-800-288-4677)

Because of the dynamic nature of the Internet, any web addresses or links contained in this book may have changed since publication and may no longer be valid. The views expressed in this work are solely those of the author and do not necessarily reflect the views of the publisher, and the publisher hereby disclaims any responsibility for them.

Any people depicted in stock imagery provided by Thinkstock are models, and such images are being used for illustrative purposes only.

Certain stock imagery © Thinkstock.

ISBN: 978-1-4502-9279-5 (sc)
ISBN: 978-1-4502-9278-8 (dj)
ISBN: 978-1-4502-9277-1 (ebk)

Library of Congress Control Number: 2011901440

Printed in the United States of America

iUniverse rev. date: 1/31/2011

Contents

PART 1

THE LEGEND

Chapter 1

Ella paced back and forth impatiently. How much longer would they be? It annoyed her that she was now waiting for them! If this was so important, what was taking them so long? What were her parents doing?

She stopped pacing long enough to take another quick look in the mirror. If it weren't bad enough having to wait, she also had her hair up, and it was driving her crazy. Just for something to do, she tightened the ribbon securing her long, golden-brown hair. Her hair was so long it nearly covered her entire back. She usually kept her hair down like most fairies her age, but her mother insisted she tie it up for this meeting. Ella wasn't looking forward to this meeting at all, but she had no choice but to go; after all, it had been arranged for her sake!

All this fuss over her, because her parents were worried about her safety. Just thinking about it made her feel ill. Ella closed her eyes, took a big breath, and then let it out slowly. She felt like the entire situation was getting blown way out of proportion. She couldn't understand why such a fuss was being made; she was still the same fairy on the inside.

She hoped this meeting would clear up some of the misunderstanding and ease her parents' minds. Maybe then they could all get back to their normal lives. The meeting was being held at the village bower, a large, open building built on the ground. In fact, it was the only building in their fairy village that was built on the ground. Located on the very edge of the village's north side, it was used for weekly lessons given by Story Teller and village meetings presided over by four village elders. Ella had never dreamed it would be used for the purpose to which it would be put tonight.

When her parents were finally ready, she yearned to say something about how long it had taken them, but she didn't dare, it would only cause a fight. They left their little tree hut without a word and quickly flew to the village bower. Standing before the door, Ella took a moment to pretend to straighten out her cloak and dress. What she was really doing was gathering her courage. She couldn't believe how nervous she was!

With a confidence she didn't really feel, she stepped through the door. A sudden rush of familiar smells greeted her; she took a deep breath in and let them wash over her. How she loved the smell of the bower. There was the smell of the wooden benches and the grass from the floor. How grass could grow in there was something she never could figure out. There was also the smell of burning wood from the fire of eternal flame, located at the center of the bower. But what Ella loved most, though, was the smell of the herbs that were used to bring Story Teller's stories to life. With the smell of the herbs came the familiar sense of calm and well being that came along with entering the bower. Ella realized she needed that sense of calmness right now more than ever.

At the back of the bower awaited Story Teller and the four elders. One of the elders beckoned Ella and her parents to approach with a wave of her hand. As Ella started to move toward them, she felt her father's hand grab hers and give a small squeeze. Looking up at him, she gave him a nervous smile.

It was Story Teller, in her light, musical voice, who spoke first. "Come, little one; come forward into the light so that we might see you better." Story Teller was a good family friend, and her familiar voice helped alleviate some of the tension.

Ella stepped forward. Story Teller smiled as Ella approached; she wasn't much taller than Ella. No one in the village knew for sure how old Story Teller was, but Ella had heard her parents say they knew her to be at least six hundred years old. You wouldn't know it to look at her, her looks revealed nothing—she appeared to be about the same age as Ella's parents. Story Teller had a small round face and dark brown—almost black—hair down to her ankles; she was, in fact, quite beautiful. In truth, all of Ella's clan were beautiful. Story Teller was just exceptionally so.

Ella felt a little shaky standing in front of Story Teller and the elders. This meeting was about the blue streaks that ran through her wings. All the others in their clan had silver wings, and so did Ella—at first. In the last few months, though, her wings had started to get small, glittering, light-blue streaks through their delicate centers. Fairies' wings weren't unlike those of a dragonfly. The wing structure consisted of two top wings and two bottom wings that connected in the center, except they ran up and down instead of sticking out to the side. The blue streaks had started in the bottom portions of her wings, but now blue ran through both top and bottom. Her mother told her that others had had blue streaks running through their wings, but that the blue faded over time. Unfortunately for Ella, the blue hadn't faded; it steadily grew larger in area and much brighter. Now the streaks shot right through to the edges of her wings and would slightly glow when it was dark. The glow or glitter of the blue was something that this or any other clan had never seen. With the stories of blue-winged fairies still being told, Ella now found herself shunned by her friends. For this reason, Ella's mother had decided that talking to the elders would be the best course of action.

Ella looked up at Story Teller, unsure if she was supposed to say something or just wait. She decided to wait. Story Teller looked at her closely for a moment and then spoke very quietly. "It always amazes me how much you look like your mother, but you have your father's blue eyes. I always envied you for the color of your eyes." Story Teller winked at Ella, but then she became serious.

"Perhaps you should show us what it is that has brought you before us tonight. Would you mind if we see your wings, Ella?"

Well, of course she minded. Everyone was making such a big deal about the blue in her wings that she didn't like anyone seeing them. But she couldn't exactly say that, now could she? With a nod, Ella removed her cloak and let her small, delicate wings unfold. The bottom wings hit just a little past her knees, and the top wings reached just a little above her head. Ella turned slowly so her back faced the adults.

The elders started to murmur. Ella felt Story Teller's small hand on her shoulder, gently pushing her toward the center of the bower, where the fire crackled. "So, little one," Story Teller said quietly, "it is true, then. This makes you a very special little fairy. We must talk about some things, you and I. Have you ever heard the entire story about the legend of the Blue Wings?"

"Not all of it. I only know what everyone else knows. The Blue Wings were evil and tried to destroy the Silver Wings." Ella paused and then asked, "I'm not sure why there's blue in my wings, but because it seems to be such a big deal, maybe we could find a way to remove it? I know it upsets my parents and I'm not really thrilled about it myself." Ella's voice was a little shaky. Her mother put her hand on her shoulder in silent support.

Story Teller smiled at the spirited little fairy. "Well, little one, you are different, and being different isn't always easy. As I've already said, the blue in your wings makes you special, very special. We can't change the color, because the blue is there for a reason. The blue is your destiny! You should know that the stories you've heard about the Blue Wings are based on fear."

A stunned murmur came from the elders. Story Teller turned for a moment to look at them but quickly looked back at Ella. She continued, "It has never been very clear to me why there is such hatred for the Blue Wings." Story Teller looked at Ella's parents. "I think everyone needs to hear my story; it's a story I haven't told in a very long time. I felt it was best left in the past. It seems I was wrong, and now it must be told again. This legend, all these years later, has become a part of Ella. Please come and sit by the fire with me." As they moved toward the fire, Story Teller grabbed her leather bag of herbs and sat down beside Ella. Ella's parents sat behind their daughter.

Everything became quiet as Story Teller removed some herbs from her pouch to throw into the fire. The fire shot straight up and then slowly came back down. A shadowy picture started to emerge just above the flame.

Chapter 2

Story Teller, in her musical voice, began to tell her story. The picture above the flames became sharp and clear, just like a movie playing on a screen.

"It was so very long ago. Some believe the Blue Wings were the first fairies to ever cross the spiritual dimensions. They were the first to live happily in the spaces between the fairy world and the human world. Our world, the between space, is so similar to both the fairy world and the human world that it would be difficult to tell the difference among the three. The Blue Wings lived here for hundreds of years, neither bothered by nor bothering either world. They lived in complete harmony with all that was around them."

The picture above the flames showed a group of fairies with blue wings moving about the forest. The first thing Ella noticed about them was that they all looked extremely happy.

"After a time, the first Silver Wing clan crossed the dimension to live in the between spaces, as well. The clans knew of each other but, for the most part, left each other alone, learning to coexist. The Blue Wings had come to this dimension because the fairy world had questioned their blue wings. They also knew the Silver Wings feared their differences, just as they feared anything that was different or unknown to them. It wasn't just their wing color;

it was the Blue Wings' abilities and powers that truly marked the differences between them. Silver Wing fairies are each blessed with one gift or ability. Blue Wing fairies, however, are each born with all the fairy gifts. Some believe the Blue Wings have gifts that the Silver Wings haven't even heard of."

Story Teller looked at Ella. "The Blue Wing fairies were a much more advanced group of fairies. They were stronger, wiser, and far more attuned to their abilities. In the end, what it came down to was that the Silver Wings were jealous of the Blue Wings' many abilities." Story Teller again winked at Ella.

"The first Silver Wings called themselves the Clan Stafford. As time went on, other Silver Wing clans came forth from the fairy world. It is not known exactly why so many clans moved, but it is said there had been great unrest in the fairy world. The new Silver Wing king was not a kind king. Soon there were as many as twenty different Silver Wing clans living near the Blue Wings. The Silver Wing clans were small, but, in comparison, the Blue Wings were a smaller clan yet.

"As time went on, the differences between the Silver Wings and the Blue Wings became far more apparent. The Silver Wings realized just how much more advanced the Blue Wings really were. Because of this, the Silver Wings started to question the Blue Wings' presence here. It didn't matter that the Blue Wings were the first to live here or that it was because of the Blue Wings that the Silver Wings could cross over into this world. These were not important issues to the Silver Wings. What did matter was where the Blue Wings came from, why they had moved here, and whether there could be more of them somewhere. If one of the Silver Wings had simply gone to the Blue Wings and asked these questions, the Blue Wings would have happily answered. The Blue Wings, a peaceful, spiritual group of fairies, had nothing to hide. However, fear of the Blue Wings was so great that it prevented anyone from the Silver Wing clans from going to speak to them."

Story Teller pointed to the pictures above the fire. "The most interesting thing was that the Blue Wings had tried to help the Silver Wings on many occasions." The fire showed several Blue Wing fairies helping the Silver Wings with various tasks.

"The Blue Wings knew their motives for helping were questioned yet continued to help despite this. The Blue Wings advised the Silver Wings on better ways of constructing their tree huts and on what herbs could be used for general health and healing. But the more the Blue Wings tried to help, the more the Silver Wings feared them.

"Not understanding why the Silver Wings reacted as they did, the Blue Wings felt it would be best if they pulled away from the Silver Wings. A clan meeting of the Blue Wings was called, and the problem was discussed. The Blue Wings sadly agreed it would be best if all association with the Silver Wings ended. Also, for their own clan's safety, the Blue Wings would cloak themselves from the Silver Wings."

Story Teller shook her head in dismay. "Things could have been so much better for all of us if the Silver Wings had not let jealousy and fear rule their hearts!" Story Teller let out a little sigh. "The Blue Wings hoped that discontinuing their association with the Silver Wings would help diminish some of their fears. For most of the Silver Wings, it did help a little. Regrettably, one Silver Wing fairy from the Stafford clan, Jeddah, felt this was far worse for all Silver Wings. Now their enemy was not only unknown but also unseen. If you don't know your enemy's abilities or your enemy's whereabouts, then shouldn't that be cause for greater unrest and fear? How do you protect yourself if you don't know where your enemy is because you can't see them?

"Jeddah went from village to village discussing his fears with clan elders and any other fairy who would listen. In each village, he sowed the seeds of doubt and spread the flames of fear and hate for the Blue Wings. Jeddah then arranged to have the elders from each Silver Wing clan meet and strategize a way to end the Blue Wings' potential threat. Not all the elders felt a threat existed, but with so many more voting against them, their words were not heard. A plan was made, and any elder against this plan of action was warned to stay out of the situation—or else the same fate awaiting the Blue Wings would befall them and theirs. Nothing could be done or said to deter this course of action, and the fate of the Blue Wings was sealed."

The picture above the flames started to fade.

"How can one fairy sway so many? I don't understand why." Ella was shocked.

"We were a young people then. The Blue Wings were so much more advanced that they were seen as a threat. I don't really understand it, either."

"I'm young. I don't want to hurt others because they're different!" Ella said.

"Not young in age, Ella. They were young in growth and understanding."

"What happened to the Blue Wings?"

"I was just getting to that. You should prepare yourself, Ella. This part of my story is going to be a little upsetting for you."

Chapter 3

"Two weeks later a small army of Silver Wings was sent into the forest to surround the area where they believed the Blue Wings' village was located. Five young Silver Wing fairies were sent into a small clearing and told to yell and cry for the Blue Wings' help. Before long, several Blue Wings entered the clearing, and the young Silver Wings had a story to tell them when they came. They told the Blue Wings they feared for their own lives because they'd gone against the Silver Wings' plans; they wanted to warn the Blue Wing elder about the threat against them. Those five fairies were taken into the Blue Wing village. The Blue Wing elder and the rest of the Blue Wing fairies gathered around the outdoor fire to hear the tale of the Silver Wings. Soon after this, the Silver Wing warriors entered the village and cut off all means of retreat for the Blue Wings.

"The Blue Wings were rounded up and put into a small hut that had been built in the middle of the forest, away from other villages. The Silver Wings had built it there to execute their plan. The small hut had been bound with the strongest magic the Silver Wings could conjure, which prevented anyone who entered the hut from exiting.

"Of course, the Silver Wings' magic alone was not enough. They had to borrow magic from others. They went to the witch on the hill, the elves, the gnomes, and the goblins. When asked why they needed this magic, they said they had to drive off a very powerful unknown enemy, an enemy who threatened their very existence. All who were asked, except for the witch, offered to help the Silver Wings drive off this evil. The Silver Wings declined their help, explaining that they would not ask their friends to put themselves in such danger. The truth was, the Silver Wings didn't want any of the others finding out why they really needed their magic.

"The Blue Wings understood they were in danger. First they tried to free themselves; then they tried to use their own magic to counter the Silver Wings. It wouldn't work, of course. With the extra magic the Silver Wings had borrowed, the spell was much too strong. The Blue Wings tried reasoning with the Silver Wings, but the Silver Wings would not be swayed. The Silver Wings had already judged them guilty and were ready to terminate their existence.

"At sunset that evening, the oldest, strongest fairies of each Silver Wing clan came forward as a group. They gathered in a circle, with the door of the hut directly in front of them but at a safe distance away. The oldest of these elders carried a large leather satchel; inside the satchel was a very old, fragile book bound in leather. It was the most powerful book the fairies knew of: the Book of the Dead. All fairies knew of the book, but very few had ever seen it. Because of its power, the book was always kept hidden."

Ella watched the story take shape above the fire, her heart racing as she waited to hear what the Silver Wings would do.

"The Book of the Dead was held by two of the elders at the center of the circle, while the remaining elders, encircling them, began to chant. They chanted the same string of words over and over, getting faster and louder each time. Soon the sky clouded over, and bolts of lightning hit the ground close to where they stood. A great wind started to blow, and with it came a sound so shrill it could be heard throughout the forest. The ground began to shake, and small cracks started to form below the hut, growing larger and larger with each passing moment. A tiny cloud began to form directly above the hut. It pulled dirt and debris into itself and, at the same time, started to move in a slow circular motion, like a stationary tornado. Gaining speed and size with each passing second, the cloud and everything in it began circling the hut. In mere moments, there was so much dirt and debris circling the hut that it couldn't even be seen! The cracks in the earth that had started out small began to grow, and from them a sudden beam of blinding light, accompanied by a loud creaking sound, zoomed out. The light and sound lasted for just a moment and then disappeared.

"Sudden silence followed, and nothing could be heard except the elders' quiet chant. Soon they stopped as well. When the dust settled and the sun came out from behind a cloud, everything appeared to be as it was before. There was only one change. There was no longer a hut; the hut and its occupants had been wiped out."

Chapter 4

The picture above the flames faded and disappeared with Story Teller's last words. Complete silence fell inside the bower; no one spoke for several minutes. Ella felt sick to her stomach; tears ran down her face. She could hardly believe what she'd seen. Of course it had to be true; otherwise the fire couldn't show the images. The fire would produce pictures only of actual past events; it was like a journal, with pictures instead of words. The images above the fire did not, could not, lie.

Ella had never felt shame before, yet the shame she felt at that moment for her ancestors was overwhelming. How had such a horrific act of cruelty been allowed to happen? Why hadn't the others tried to stop it? It seemed there were more questions than answers now, and she wasn't sure she really wanted to know more anyway!

Ella looked around; everyone had clearly been affected by the story. Her mother moved up to sit beside her and took her hand. Ella was grateful for her mother's comfort.

Story Teller began to speak. "I'm sure this wasn't easy for you to hear. It's always difficult for me to tell this tale; perhaps that's why I haven't done so for such a long time. Unfortunately, my tale isn't over; there's more you must hear."

"I don't want to hear anymore!" Ella sobbed. Ella's mother released her hand and wrapped her arm around her shoulders, pulling her close.

Story Teller gave Ella a sympathetic look. "I'm sorry, Ella, but you must hear the whole story." She gave Ella a moment before she continued.

"After the demise of the Blue Wings, no Silver Wing entered the Blue Wings' village. Even if they had tried, they couldn't have, because a protection spell had been placed over the village. Some said the Blue Wings put a spell on it, and others thought that the spirits of the Blue Wings lived on there. It didn't matter what the reasons were. All that mattered was that no Silver Wing fairy dared to try to find that village again. This was how the story was told to me. The village wasn't looked upon for hundreds and hundreds of years.

"It was by accident that the first fairy came upon and entered the Blue Wings' village. This fairy hadn't heard of the Blue Wing fairies and didn't know the story. He was sent out to find a new location for another village to be built. When he found the deserted village, he was shocked. He said it was the most beautiful village he had ever seen, and he believed the people who'd inhabited the village had only just left. Everything in the village remained as it once was, clean, neat, and tidy, providing no evidence of a long absence. When he looked around, he found parts of a journal inside one of the tree huts and a few other journals in the village bower. The journal found in the tree hut wasn't complete; it contained just a few entries. He started to read the partial journal and saw the date of the last entry. Imagine his surprise when he realized it'd been over five hundred years since the last fairy lived there.

"It's not known what happened to the rest of the journal, and it was never found. The full journals contained accounts of the Blue Wings' daily life, but the partial journal held several entries of interest. Those entries pertain to you, Ella, although no one knew this at the time."

Ella's head was resting on her mother's shoulder while Story Teller was speaking. At Story Teller's last words, she jerked her head up so fast it made her dizzy. "I don't understand. How could they write about me so long ago?"

"No names were written. The journal told a story and contained a prediction."

Ella's confusion shone in her eyes. Story Teller looked down at her and smiled. "Don't worry, little one. Soon it will all become clear."

Ella could only nod.

Story Teller continued. "The last pages told of a young Blue Wing fairy who hadn't ended his association with the Silver Wings, as the rest of his clan had. He'd been seeing a young fairy from the Stafford clan and, in fact, had fallen deeply in love with her. They knew their relationship would not have been looked upon favorably by either of their families, so they continued to see each other secretly. During their affair, the young girl found herself with child. This prompted the boy to go to his village's elder and tell him of their love. The boy told the elder he and the girl were going to sneak away and live out their lives in the human world. The boy felt this was the only way he could ensure the safety of his new family. This was what was written by the Blue Wing elder."

Story Teller gave Ella a sad smile. "Some speculated that the girl went to her family as well, so that when she left, they would not worry. Some believe that Jeddah, being from the Stafford clan, somehow heard of the young girl's story. It was her love affair that fueled his hatred for the Blue Wings and sparked his quest to wipe them out. Jeddah believed that the young Blue Wing fairy had cast some kind of spell over the girl and that it was the spell that had caused the girl to behave so horridly. If the girl had been in her right mind, she wouldn't have chosen to mate with the enemy."

Ella's mind swam with the possibilities this new information brought. To think that when she'd first come to the bower, her biggest concern had been the blue in her wings! She had to force herself to refocus on the story being told.

"The Blue Wing elder didn't write anything in the journal for several days after that last entry." Story Teller looked again at Ella. "We do know that the young lovers never got their chance to run away together. When that final day came for all the Blue Wing fairies, the young boy was with them. The Blue Wing elder knew something bad was going to happen. That was evident in the next journal entry." Story Teller took a deep breath before she spoke the Blue Wing elder's words:

"'Great danger is coming our way. For this reason, I must ensure the prophecy be written. If, for some reason, something should happen to our clan, and I am all but sure something will, it should be known that our bloodline, the blood of the Blue Wings, will not die with us. The young Silver Wing girl will give birth to the child who is a descendent of the Blue Wings. This child will not be born with blue wings; she will have her mother's silver wings. No one will know that the blood of the Blue Wings runs through this child, and this knowledge will not come to light for many centuries. This knowledge will come forth only when these pages are found. Too much time will have passed for anyone to trace back the exact bloodlines through which the Blue Wings' blood runs. It will have passed through many clans, and there won't be any way of knowing who will pass our blood and who will not.

"'Many more centuries will pass before our descendent will be born. A child will be born to a couple who will produce only one heir. This child will bear silver wings, but only at first. In time, the blue of our wings will begin to show. This child will come to know that it is the blood of the Blue Wings that courses through her, not only in color but in strength and knowledge, too. All the Blue Wings' gifts and powers this child will hold within. She alone will hold the key to making all that was once wrong, right again, bringing with it forgiveness and love. She will help answer all the unanswered questions and reestablish all creatures' lost trust.

"'To this child I speak: Come forth, my daughter, with pride. With our blood comes a promise. You will never be alone, nor should you have any fear. It matters not where destiny takes you. Look to the four elements—air, water, fire, and earth. Look within and you shall find the fifth element, spirit. Within these elements, you will find that your ancestors walk with you and give you strength.

"'Your life will not be easy or without risk. Someone will watch over you, protect you, and help guide you, your unshakable guardian throughout your life. Take care, our young child fairy, for soon your destiny will take you to places you thought you would never have to go. No matter what, always remember that you are not alone.'"

Ella looked at Story Teller. "You think he's talking about me? It can't be me! This whole thing is crazy!"

Chapter 5

This was crazy, so crazy it had to be a dream. That was it! This was a dream, and she would wake up soon. Ella's mother took her hand. Ella was surprised to find that her mother was shaking a little. When she looked over at her father, she saw that his crystal-blue eyes were troubled; his dark face was now as pale as the white daisies that grew in the meadow. At that moment, she realized this was really happening; she was not going to wake up from it.

Ella looked at Story Teller and softly asked, "You think I'm the child the Blue Wing elder was writing about?"

Story Teller nodded. "Yes, Ella, you are that child. And that makes you incredibly special. It also puts you in some danger, I'm afraid. When word spreads, and we both know it will, how will our people respond? I would like to believe that over all these centuries the Silver Wings have grown and won't react to you as they did to your ancestors. Yet there will always be someone who will be guided by their fears and react accordingly."

Ella looked at everyone in the room. All the elders had their heads down, and her parents looked a little shell-shocked.

"Perhaps there's been a mistake. Maybe my wings will turn back to silver and I'm not really the child from the Blue Wing elder's story. "

Story Teller stood up. "You are the one, and if you look deep within, I know you'll see it's true." Story Teller turned and started to walk toward a small door at the back of the bower. Behind this door was a small waiting room for visitors who came to meet with an elder.

As Story Teller walked she spoke again. "It would seem we aren't the only magical beings who record and remember the past. Someone came this evening, just before our meeting. He has a story to tell you, Ella, a story we all need to hear. There's someone I would like you to meet." Story Teller pulled on the handle, and the door slowly opened.

At first, Ella couldn't see anyone; there wasn't enough light inside the small room. She wasn't sure who she thought would be on the other side of the door, but nothing could have prepared her for who it was. The creature behind the door stepped forward into the light.

Chapter 6

Standing before them was the largest wolf any of them had ever seen. Ella knew she should stand to meet their guest, but she wasn't sure her shaking legs would hold her up. After a few tries, she did manage to get to her feet. Her parents stood as well.

She could see the wolf more clearly as he walked slowly toward her, into the light. Most of his fur was a shiny charcoal black. All four of his paws had shades of gray around them, making him look like he was wearing socks. There were light-gray patches inside his ears and just above his eyes. Around his eyes was a thin strip of white fur, as though someone had taken white paint and painted a perfect oval around them, which only enhanced his eye color. He would have been quite a handsome wolf except for the battle scars he wore on his muzzle, chest, and legs. Ella was sure he had many more scars, but she couldn't see them under his thick, dark fur. The color of his eyes stood out most. They were the clearest, brightest light blue Ella had ever seen. She was sure those eyes could fill with light and happiness when the wolf felt so inclined, but right now they were dark and cold.

The wolf stopped just in front of Ella and leaned in to sniff her; Ella stood rock-still. She knew for certain that this was the largest wolf she'd ever seen. If he was hungry right now, she would be only a very small snack for him, leaving the rest of her clan

22

for the main course. Surely this wolf could smell the fear pouring off of her!

At that moment, the wolf did something so unexpected that Ella heard her father gasp. The wolf smiled! She was right—his eyes did fill with light. The wolf bent one leg and kneeled down, lowering his large head as he did. Holding his position in front of her, he lifted his head and spoke. "Princess of the Blue Wings, it is my humble privilege to kneel before you." He then rose to a standing position.

Ella's entire body vibrated from the wolf's voice; that was how low and deep it was. It was the kind of voice you didn't just hear but also felt. A strange sensation passed over and through Ella's body. In all her life, she'd never felt anything like it. It felt like all the power this wolf held passed to her and then passed back to the wolf, and it made her dizzy. She felt she'd known him all her life, even though they'd just met. A very strong connection had passed between them, and the wolf smiled knowingly.

"Princess, let me introduce myself. My name is Brogan, and I am from the warrior clan of Kallan. I have come a long way to see you, and I have much to tell you. First, however, I must express how honored I am to be your guardian." The wolf bowed his head a second time.

Ella must have been in shock, because she was slow to pick up on his last words. Not until her father spoke did it fully register.

Ella's father said, "Guardian? You are to be her guardian?"

"What in heaven's name for?" Ella's mother said.

"Guardian?" Ella was proud of herself; her voice sounded almost normal. She stood a little taller and tried very hard not to come across as a frightened, needy, nerdy little fairy. "I'm not sure what you mean by 'guardian,' Mr. Brogan, but I don't think I really need one." She was a little overwhelmed.

Brogan glanced at Story Teller and then turned his eyes back to Ella. "It would please me greatly if you would just call me Brogan. Your circumstances have changed, Princess. You must now be concerned for your safety from all fairies, even the ones you know. I understand that, at this point, you do not fully understand the importance of your existence, though I do intend to enlighten you on this point. Do you believe that my being here today, at this exact time, is coincidence? If you do, then please let me assure you that it's not! There is no such thing as coincidences. This was predetermined centuries ago. It's not just for your sake I stand here before you."

Brogan looked around the room, as though just realizing they were not alone. Putting his head down and closing his eyes, he took a deep breath. Then he looked up and spoke to everyone who stood around the fire. "As I said, there is much I must tell you. Before I start, perhaps it might be best if we all sat by the fire." Even before he finished speaking, he sat down and leaned in toward the fire. "I must apologize." He glanced briefly at each fairy. "I have been traveling nonstop for several days to get here, and I must say it is rather nice to be seated before a nice warm fire." The warrior wolf chuckled.

The sound of laughter wasn't something Ella had expected to hear from the monster wolf, but she suspected his laughter had been caused by the look on her face as she watched him sit before the fire.

Unsure what to do, Ella looked to her parents. Her mother took her hand and moved them both closer to the wolf. She pulled Ella down into a sitting position. Ella's father sat on her other side. "Perhaps you should tell us your story, warrior," Ella's father said.

Chapter 7

Brogan waited to speak until everyone was seated. "As I have mentioned, I am from the warrior clan of Kallan, which has existed for many centuries. We are trained from birth in the ways of a warrior. My being here tonight is no coincidence; it was prearranged many centuries ago. We have been waiting for this day for a very long time."

Brogan kept his eyes on Ella. "Our clan has always kept careful records. One record has always been of the utmost importance—the record of our visit from Eamon, the elder of the Blue Wings. He came to us exactly one year to the day before the decimation of the Blue Wing clan. He knew what was in store for the Blue Wings, and he knew the Silver Wings would rise up against them to wipe them out. The warriors of our clan offered our protection to him and his clan, but Eamon refused our help. He was there to secure not his own protection but the protection of a future Blue Wing fairy. That, of course, is you." Brogan nodded at Ella.

Brogan's eyes stayed locked with Ella's as he continued. "Eamon gave the leader of our clan all the information we would need to carry out our duties. This information was very precise. We were told when you would be born and who your parents would be. There was information on the clan you would belong to and even what your parents would name you."

Brogan stopped for moment to let this information sink in. He was very much aware that what Ella was hearing would seem very strange and farfetched. He himself had been unsure if, after all those years, the Blue Wing princess would really exist.

"It was written that a meeting would be held on this day, and a Kallan warrior should be in attendance to explain to you the importance of your future. I am that warrior, and it is my privilege to be your guardian." Brogan bowed his head slightly before he continued.

"Your birth was the trigger for many future changes. Much has changed over the years, and it was the Blue Wings' hope that with those changes your existence would not pose such a threat to others. Your birth has started a ripple effect in this world. You are the first pure-blood Blue Wing born to this world in over seven centuries, and you will lead others. You must learn a great deal before you can lead your people. Although much has changed, some will still see you as a threat. They will look to the past and want to do to you what was done to your ancestors. If something should happen to you, the blood of the Blue Wings will disappear. There will be no other birth of a pure-blood Blue Wing ever again, and the bloodline will end. Keeping you safe is the only way to ensure the Blue Wings' existence."

Brogan looked at everyone in the room and saw shock in their eyes. One of the elders looked like she might be sick. He looked at Ella again to see if she understood what he'd said. He couldn't read her eyes, though, because she was violently shaking her head. Then he heard her say, very quietly, one word: "*No!*"

Chapter 8

Ella felt like she'd just run around the village several times. She was struggling to catch her breath; she was sweating, shaking, and having a hard time focusing. She was certain only that she no longer wanted to be here and that she didn't want to hear anything more from anyone. The only word she could form was *no*.

Ella sat for a moment in the silent room. Everyone was staring at her like she had grown a second head. What was going on? One of the elders was bent over, taking very deep breaths. She hadn't thought her saying "no" would get this kind of reaction. The staring was making her very uncomfortable. Perhaps she should say something.

"I am very sorry, Brogan, that you traveled so long to get here, but you must understand that I honestly believe you've made a mistake. I don't think I am the fairy you seek."

"I know this must be very hard for you, but it's you who must understand—there is no mistake!" Brogan looked carefully at Ella. "You are the fairy I have traveled so far to see, and you are the descendent of the Blue Wings. If my words do not convince you, then perhaps your wings will."

Ella looked back at her wings and received a jolt of shock. Now she understood everyone's reaction. Ella heard her mother quietly saying a fairy prayer and her father trying to reassure her that everything would be all right. Ella's stomach churned, and she could feel her heartbeat in her head. She took some very deep breaths to keep from getting sick or fainting.

At some point between the time Brogan came in and now, her wings had turned the most brilliant, unusual colors of blue, with no sign whatsoever of silver. Her wings were so bright, in fact, that they looked like they glowed from within. It almost looked like someone had poured glitter dust on them. You couldn't actually name the color of blue; all variations of the color were swirled together. Ella was sure they would, indeed, glow in the dark. Never had she seen anything like it before; and, judging by everyone else's reactions, no one else had, either. The only one not staring was Brogan. She couldn't believe she hadn't noticed such a change happening. They were so bright it was almost impossible not to notice them. They were almost as bright as the fire.

All she could say was, "Oh, my."

"It was written in our records that your wings will glow only when you are having strong emotions. They will not always be so bright, and eventually you will be able to control it, but you must come into your powers first. There's much for you to learn." Brogan directed his next words at Ella's parents. "There will be much for all of us to learn."

Ella's parents moved in closer beside her. Her mother was silently crying. Ella squeezed her mother's hand and then let go.

Everything was so overwhelming, and she felt very tired, both physically and emotionally. "I'm not sure how this can be. How is it that I have Blue Wing blood running through me? How can I be a pure-blood Blue Wing when both my parents are Silver Wings?"

"That's a good question. I can't answer it, but I can give you a theory. It's believed the Blue Wing bloodline in you dominates because both your parents have a high concentration of Blue Wing blood running through them. My clan believes that this blood was passed to you and that the Blue Wings' blood is stronger than the Silver Wings'. As you grew, the Blue Wings' blood over took or altered the Silver Wings' blood. Your blood is now that of the Blue Wings." Brogan smiled at Ella. "It isn't entirely understood, but you are to be gifted with all the Blue Wings' abilities."

Ella looked at her parents. "That doesn't really answer the question."

Brogan shrugged. "I'm sorry, but that's all I know. The only thing that matters at this point is that you are a Blue Wing!"

Ella sighed. "So what happens now?"

Story Teller approached Ella, kneeled down, and put her hands on Ella's shoulders. "You will stay with your parents for now. You must have your ceremony before anything else can happen. The only change is that Brogan will stay with you. He is your guardian, which means he remains with you always. He will watch over you, protect you, teach you, and help you along this unknown path. You should know that I will always be here for you as well, and if you need anything or want me to help you in any way, never be afraid to ask, even if it's just to have someone listen to you." Story Teller kissed Ella on the forehead.

As Story Teller stepped back, Brogan stepped forward. "One more thing must be done tonight. Eamon, the Blue Wing elder, left something for you. He was adamant that you and you alone receive it. Could you stand up, please?"

Ella stood.

"No other fairy hand but yours must touch it. This was made very clear by the Blue Wing elder." Brogan walked toward Ella until he was standing directly in front of her. He then bowed his head so she could reach it. "You will find it around my neck." He took a small step closer, indicating that Ella would have to take it off for him.

She hadn't seen anything around his neck, so she wasn't sure what to expect. She moved her small fingers through his fur until she felt a chain. His fur was extremely soft, which surprised her. She followed the chain down, which didn't take long because the chain was rather tight around his large neck, and she felt something round hanging from it. Grasping the round object, she carefully pulled up on the chain. Brogan's head was so large that removing the chain was difficult. She got the chain over his eyes, but when she continued to pull, it folded Brogan's ears forward. At this point, she felt very self-conscious and awkward, and her hands were shaking. Trying very hard to be gentle, she pulled each ear out from under the chain, until finally she was able to pull the chain free.

She held the chain and amulet in the palm of her hand so she could see them better. The amulet looked like a round, shiny glass rock surrounded by delicate gold weave; the chain itself was delicate and gold. The glass was the same colors as her wings. It was one of the most beautiful things she had ever seen. A tingling sensation started in her hand and traveled quickly throughout her body. She had a feeling of familiarity when she looked at the necklace, although she knew she had never seen it before. This was meant for her.

She looked up at Brogan, and he nodded. Ella placed the necklace around her neck. The chain, which had been so tight around Brogan's neck, was quite long on her; the amulet hung almost to her tummy. She would have to shorten the chain.

She studied the amulet again. For a moment, she thought she saw the colors swirl around. She closed her eyes and opened them again. It must have been the way the firelight was reflected on the glass. As she continued to look at it, a strange feeling swept over her, like finally finding a piece of yourself that you weren't really aware was missing. It was the strangest feeling! Of course, this had also been the strangest night.

If only the amulet could have shown her how strange the next day would be.

PART 2

LEARNING CURVE

Chapter 9

Normally, when Ella woke up, she would get out of bed right away and prepare to face the day. This morning was different. This morning, Ella just lay there with her eyes closed, thinking about everything that had happened the night before. She thought, *you would think I would feel different somehow*—but she didn't feel any different! It felt like any other morning on any other day.

She rolled onto her tummy and stretched her wings. Turning her head a little, she took a look and was flooded with a queasy feeling. She'd hoped last night had been only a dream. She'd had a small hope that when she woke today her wings would still be mostly silver; but they were still several different shades of blue. Ella buried her face in the pillow. *Well, fairy farts,* she thought.

After finally getting up, Ella got dressed and went downstairs. She said good morning to her parents and then walked onto the veranda of their tree hut. There he was, her wolf guardian, lying at the base of their tree hut, looking even larger in the morning light.

"Good morning, little one!" Brogan stood up and stretched. "You slept well, I hope."

Without thinking, Ella muttered under her breath, "Well, double fairy farts!"

Brogan looked up at her with confusion. "Excuse me?"

"Oh, I'm so sorry. It's just that there was a small part of me that was hoping you wouldn't really be here and last night was just a dream. No offense."

"None taken, I guess. Although denial won't change what's happening." Brogan watched Ella fly down.

"It's hard to be in denial when you're standing here talking to me." Ella smiled. "So now what happens? What am I supposed to do?"

"I'm not sure. What do fairies your age normally do on a morning like this?" Brogan gave Ella a lopsided grin.

Ella wasn't sure why, but that smile really irritated her. He seemed to be mocking her. "Is that the way you always smile?"

"No." Brogan's lopsided smile got even bigger. "Why? Does it bother you?"

"Of course not. I was just wondering." She sure wasn't going to admit to him it did.

"So what would you do today if I wasn't here?"

"Lately, I haven't been doing much. Since my wings started to turn blue, most of the fairies my age haven't wanted much to do with me. I don't even want to know what their reactions will be when they see my wings now." Ella rolled her eyes to cover the pain she felt.

"How do the adults react to you?"

"Some are still good to me, but most of the village stays away from me now. I hear them whisper when I go by. The odd one will still say hi, but I think they are just being courteous for my parents' sake. I do most things on my own. Sometimes my best friend, Astral, will hang out with me. It's not like it used to be between us, though. It's hard for her, too, I guess."

"It matters not what others think. You must be strong and remain positive. I know that's easier said than done, but remaining true to yourself is what will get you through the hard times. Trust me; things will get better."

"When the fairies of this village see my wings now, things won't get better. I can't be in denial about that. Then there's you.

How do you think others will react when they see you standing at my side?"

Brogan lowered his head for a moment. "It's for your safety that I'm here. Tell me about your upcoming Fire Ceremony."

Ella shook her head. There was no point trying to explain that his presence would cause more strain between her and her clansmen. She wasn't even sure it mattered now that her wings were totally blue. She sat down and leaned against the base of the tree-hut tree.

"My ceremony is tomorrow at the village bower." Ella didn't look at Brogan. She looked at the sky and watched the clouds move in their slow, carefree way.

Brogan sat down beside her. "What happens at this ceremony? What's its purpose?"

"The fire acknowledges your coming of age when you turn eighteen. It's to welcome you into being a full-fledged fairy. Astral had hers a couple of weeks ago. She came and told me about it. The keeper of the fire, Story Teller, gives you some special herbs that you throw on the fire."

"What are the herbs for?"

"Story Teller chooses them for each fairy. They are a gift to the fire for the information it gives you. First, you tell the fire your full name and the names of your parents. After you do that, the fire gives you information about yourself."

"Why wouldn't you already know these things about yourself?" Brogan looked confused. Ella smiled.

"It's information the fire has to give you. First, the fire tells you what your ability is. For example, Astral's ability is herbalist. She kind of knew that already, because she's always been good with plants and herbs."

"What do you think your ability will be?"

"I have no idea; I have talent in many areas. Normally Silver Wings are blessed only with one ability, but now that my wings are blue, I'm not sure how it'll work." Ella looked back up at the clouds.

"If you remember, you are to have all the abilities that are given to fairies. That's how it was for the Blue Wings that came before you."

"I'd forgotten about that." Ella's eyes widened. "Oh, that'll go over well with the others in my village!"

"What else will the fire tell you?"

Ella took a big breath and exhaled slowly. "Well, it tells you what your role in the village will be, which is decided based on what your ability is. Astral, because of her affinity with plants, will assist the village healer in helping the sick. The fire also tells you at what age you are to stop physically aging."

"This is why no fairy looks that old? Interesting."

"It's always been this way for fairies. Astral was told she would stop aging at twenty-nine, which she felt was a little old, but you can't change this age after the fire has stated it."

"At what age do you hope to stop aging?" Brogan watched Ella's face closely.

"I don't know. I've never really given it much thought. It doesn't matter, though, because I don't choose the age."

"This is all the fire tells you?"

"Oh, no, there are a few more things. It tells you who might be a good match for a possible life partner, but only if these possible matches live in the same village. It also tells you if you are destined to stay in this village or if it is your destiny to move. In the end, though, it is up to you to decide these last two things."

"Your friend Astral—what did the fire tell her?" Ella gave Brogan a strange look. "Well, you've told me what the fire has said about everything else. I'm curious now."

"The fire told her she had three possible life mates to choose from. Two of the three she had already been seeing. She was also told she was destined to remain in this village."

"Have you been seeing anyone from this village?"

Ella lowered her head. "No. It is difficult to date when everyone avoids you."

Brogan was just about to say something when he stopped suddenly and cocked his head to listen. "Many people are coming our way."

Ella looked up and saw a large group of fairies from her village walking toward them. "I guess we're going to find out how others react to you," Ella said.

Chapter 10

The group stopped several yards away. Ella heard them whispering and saw a few pointing at Brogan. Astral's mother, Asia, walked to the front with Astral close behind.

"I demand to see your wings, young fairy! Who is this?" Asia looked her normal angry self. As far back as Ella could remember, Asia had always looked angry. Like her daughter, she had long, straight blond hair. Unlike Astral, she had dark, angry eyes. Asia was plumper than most fairies, and, by fairy standards, she was a little short. Asia had a bad temper and took it out on her own children. She also happened to be the village gossip; nothing went on in the village that she didn't know about. So it was no surprise to Ella that Asia had found out about the previous night's meeting.

"Good morning, Asia." Ella stood up to look her friend's mother in the eye. "Let me introduce you to my guardian. Asia, this is Brogan, from the Clan Kallan."

"Your guardian? What do you need with a guardian, might I ask?" Asia said disgustedly.

Ella's parents came out onto the veranda. When they saw half the village standing below them, they flew down to their daughter's side.

Ella's mother stepped forward. "What's going on here?"

"I demand to see your daughter's wings." Asia pointed to Ella. "Did you honestly think the rest of us wouldn't find out?" Asia's voice dripped with venom.

Ella's mother looked at Asia and then at the rest of the group. "We haven't tried to hide anything from anyone. It's still early morning. Last night, Ella's wings turned completely blue. Ella, could you please show them?"

Ella looked at her mother as though she were deranged. Her mother only smiled and nodded. Ella turned around and spread her wings.

All at once there were sounds of exclamation, disgust, horror, and disbelief. Everyone started to speak at once. It was difficult to hear any one fairy speaking, but Ella heard bits and pieces of what was said, including words like *abomination, freak, unnatural, disgusting*, and *not one of us*. Ella wanted the ground to open up and swallow her.

Suddenly a deafening growl rumbled out. It was so intense that the ground actually shook. Everyone stopped talking and looked at Brogan; loud growling sounds came from the back of his throat. Very intently, he took several steps forward so that he was standing in front of Asia. Asia unconsciously took two steps back.

Ella's father took advantage of the sudden stillness. "Friends, what's going on here? This is Ella you're talking about. She was born in this village, and she has grown up here. You all know her, and you all know what kind of fairy she is. This isn't her fault! We didn't ask for this to happen, but it has. How can you turn on someone from your own village, someone you know? Is all this really necessary?"

Asia spoke. "Yes, we know you, but that doesn't change the danger Ella represents. You staying in this village will put us all at risk. Sooner or later, others will hear about her and come to see for themselves, and there will be trouble because of it. Are you willing to endanger us all?"

Having had the last word, Asia gave a signal and everyone turned to leave. Asia whispered something in her daughter's ear. Before Asia left, she looked at Ella again. "I always knew you would be the cause of great trouble! As usual, I wasn't wrong." With a disgusted shake of her head, Asia walked away with the rest of the fairies. Astral was the only one to remain. Judging by the look on her face, it seemed she thought it might have been better if she had left with the rest.

Chapter 11

Once everyone had left, Astral walked forward. She stopped when Brogan stepped in front of Ella, giving Astral a warning growl.

"Brogan, it's all right. This is my friend Astral. The one I was telling you about."

Brogan moved to the side but stayed close.

Astral put her hand on her friend's shoulder. "Nice guard dog you have." Her tone was sarcastic.

"He's not a dog; he's a warrior wolf. What was that all about?"

Astral dropped her hand. "Well, Ella, what did you think was going to happen? Did you think everyone would come running to give you a big hug and congratulate you on your nice blue wings? How come you didn't tell me about your secret meeting with the elders?"

"I didn't know about it until the last minute. Even if I had, would it have changed the outcome? No. I still don't understand what the big deal is. I'm still the same fairy I was when my wings were silver." Ella lowered her head so Astral couldn't see the tears gathering in her eyes.

"What's the big deal?" Astral's voice was cold. She gave Ella a look of pure disgust, but then she noticed that Brogan had witnessed her doing so. She stepped to the side so he couldn't see her face. "The big deal is that your wings are totally blue now. You've heard the stories, and you know what others think of the Blue Wings. You're one of them now, and you're putting not only yourself in danger but everyone else, too."

Ella had gotten control over her tears and looked Astral in the eye. "Why are you speaking to me like this? I thought you were my friend. You make it sound like I've done this on purpose or chose this for myself. You know what I think? I think you're more like your mother than you realize!" Ella was getting angry.

Astral was stunned, as Ella knew she would be. They'd been friends too long for Ella not to know how much Astral dreaded being compared to her mother.

"I'm so sorry, Ella. I didn't realize." She gave her friend a big hug. When she stepped back, she hung her head in shame. "I'm sorry. Just be careful, Ella. Whether you want it to or not, your wings turning completely blue changes things, and not for the good." Astral quickly walked away.

When Ella turned away, Brogan watched Astral send Ella a look over her shoulder that was filled with disgust and hate. She gave him the same look before flying off.

When Astral walked into the tree hut, she found her mother waiting by the door.

"Did you speak with her?"

"Yes, Mother, I did. I told her what you wanted me to tell her." Astral sat in a chair across the room. She felt confused and ashamed.

"I can't believe you'd choose the Blue Wing descendent to be your best friend. It shows what kind of fairy you really are, now, doesn't it. It's up to you to take care of this problem!"

Astral watched her mother walk away from her in disgust.

Chapter 12

Ella was lying in bed when she heard her mother calling her. She had hardly slept at all. It was the morning of her ceremony. She knew she should get up and get ready to go see Story Teller, but all she wanted to do was pull the covers over her head and go back to sleep. Better yet, she wished she could become invisible and disappear.

Suddenly, her entire body started to tingle, as though thousands of little pins were being pushed into every inch of her body. She was just about to call her mother when she heard her door open and her mother came in.

"Ella, you really have to hurry, or you're going to be late."

"Um, I'm not sure, but I think something is wrong with me. I'm not feeling right." Ella sat up and prepared to stand, but when she looked down, she realized she couldn't see herself.

Her mother was looking for Ella's good cloak and had her back to her daughter. "Ella, please, we don't have time for this. You know we can't change what today is or what will happen. No excuse will get you out of going. So please just get up and get ready!" Ella heard the frustration in her mother's voice. She watched her mother take her cloak off the shelf and shake it out, getting it ready for her to put on.

"No, really, this isn't an excuse. There's something seriously wrong. Look at me—I'm not here. Well, I am, but you can't see me." Her voice was shaking and higher pitched than usual.

Her mother looked at her. "What are you talking about?" She scanned the bed. "Ella, please, no games today. Now where are you?" Annoyance laced her mother's voice.

"That's what I'm trying to tell you! I'm right here!" To prove her point, she picked up her blanket. She could see the blanket but not her hand, only the blanket being held up in the air. Then the blanket started to fade, quickly becoming invisible. "I'm holding the blanket right now. Can you see me?"

Ella's mother gave a startled gasp. "Oh, my goodness!" She walked over to the bed and reached out to touch the spot where Ella's hand should have been. Ella felt her mother's hand grab hers. "What the good fairy has happened to you?"

"I'm not really sure. All of a sudden, my whole body started to go all tingly, and then I couldn't see myself. Have you ever seen this happen?"

"Maybe I should call Brogan; he might know what's going on. If Brogan can't help, then we will have to go see Story Teller a little earlier and see if she might know what's happening." Ella's mother glanced around the room and shook her head and then hurried off to look for Brogan.

Several minutes later, Ella heard Brogan climb the small flight of stairs and approach her room. The whole tree hut shook with each of his steps. This was the first time Brogan had been in the tree hut. He'd chosen to stay outside at night simply because he was much too big to be indoors. Plus, it was a bit of a challenge to get him up to the tree hut. He had to take several leaps using trees around the tree hut as springboards. He managed to get up to the porch the first night, but it took him several tries. Of course, fairies didn't need stairs or ladders, because they could fly. The only stairs in the house connected the lower half to the upper half, as flying indoors was a bit difficult.

Ella knew when Brogan was outside her door; she felt and heard the deep rumble of his voice. "Ella, your mother says you have a problem. Could you open the door?"

Apparently her mother had decided not to tell him what was happening. Ella slowly opened the door. Brogan walked in and looked around the room. "So, little one, what can I help you with?"

Ella reached out and touched the side of his neck as she began to speak. "It seems I might have a small problem. No one can see me."

Brogan, startled, took a small step back and scanned the area where he had heard Ella's voice. "I see! You're right. That might be a small problem."

"Do you know what's happening?"

"Yes, I believe I do." Brogan looked away, trying to hide his amusement.

Ella didn't miss the amused look. "You think this is funny?" Her voice held a small amount of hurt. "Perhaps you could share with me what's going on, so then we could both laugh about it!"

"My apologies, Princess. I don't mean to insult you. Tell me, what were you thinking about before this happened?

"I was thinking I didn't want to go to my ceremony."

"Did you think you'd like to disappear?"

"Yes, I suppose I did. I thought it would be better if I was invisible so that . . . " Ella stopped for a moment. "I think I know where you're going with this. I thought it, and it happened. One of the Blue Wings' abilities, I suppose."

Brogan chuckled. "You only need to think yourself solid again." As soon as he said this, Ella's form materialized.

"I admit I feel a little foolish, and you're not helping by laughing at me. This is all new to me, you know."

"Again, I apologize. Perhaps you don't see the humor in it now, but, in time, when you look back, you'll chuckle. I will leave you now to get ready for your ceremony. I will wait in the kitchen with your mother." Brogan chuckled again and walked out.

Ella was so embarrassed! Brogan's laughter made the entire situation that much worse. "Well, fairy farts." It was all she could think to say.

Ella's mother yelled from downstairs, "Ella, I heard that. I don't care what's going on or how old you are, you don't curse under my roof. Do you understand me, young fairy?"

"Sorry, Mother," Ella yelled back down.

She sat on her bed for a moment before she got up to get ready. *Well, isn't this an interesting day,* she thought, *and it's barely begun.* She wondered what other bizarre Blue Wing abilities she was in for!

Chapter 13

Ella couldn't understand why everyone thought what had happened to her this morning was even remotely funny. Of course, Brogan explained everything to her parents, and they both laughed! Contrary to what Brogan said, Ella didn't think she would ever look back on this morning and laugh, because it wasn't funny! Ella's father put his arm around her as they walked to the bower and apologized for laughing, but it didn't make it any easier.

When they got to the bower, Brogan filled Story Teller in on Ella's exciting morning. Story Teller didn't laugh outright, but she did smile. She also remarked on how handy being invisible could be sometimes. Ella just wasn't seeing it.

Shortly after they arrived, Ella's parents gave her a big hug and then went outside with Brogan to wait. Story Teller took her hand and led her to the fire. Ella was getting a nervous butterfly feeling in her tummy. Story Teller must have sensed it, because she gave her a reassuring hug before motioning for her to sit. Story Teller then walked over to the table and retrieved a small leather bag. She sat down across from Ella.

"So, little one, today is your day! I have to tell you, I wasn't sure if you would come to see me today. This isn't something I've ever had to worry about before." She looked at Ella. "I'm not sure what the consequences would be if you were to miss your fire ceremony. It's never happened before. So I must say that I'm extremely pleased to see you here and that I won't have to find out the consequences!" Story Teller smiled. Ella knew she was trying to lighten the mood.

"What do you think is going to happen?" Ella asked.

Story Teller's face became very serious. "Honestly, I don't know. I'm not sure how things will evolve for you. For anyone else, I could give them a good idea of what to expect. For you, I can say only that no matter what happens, you're not alone! Always remember that. You will always have your parents, me, and Brogan." Story Teller touched the top of Ella's hand. Ella smiled weakly.

"Perhaps we should begin, unless you have any questions." Story Teller looked at Ella, who shook her head. What could she possibly ask at this point? All she wanted now was to have this over and done with. Story Teller waited for a moment and then handed Ella the leather bag.

"These are the herbs you will need to throw into the fire, a mix created just for you. After you have thrown all the herbs into the fire, you will need to say your name and the names of your parents." Story Teller looked at Ella to make sure she understood. Ella nodded.

Story Teller continued, "You may have to wait for a moment; sometimes it takes the fire a little while before it tells you what you need to hear." Story Teller started to back up, but she stopped when she saw the look on Ella's face. "Don't worry, little one. I'm not going far." She smiled encouragingly and then retreated to the elders' table.

Ella waited for Story Teller to get settled before she approached the fire. She took several deep, calming breaths. *Why am I being such a little ninny?* she wondered. *Every other fairy has to do this, so what's the big deal? Okay*, she told herself, *get it together and just get it done.* Ella took several more deep breaths, closed her eyes, and took two steps forward.

She felt the warmth of the fire on her face. She opened her eyes and looked at the tiny bag she held in her left hand. It took her several tries to open the bag, because her hands were shaking so badly. Once she got the bag open, she looked back at Story Teller, who gave Ella another smile of encouragement. Ella turned back to the fire. *Well*, she thought, *here we go!*

With her hands still shaking, Ella poured the herbs into her right hand and then threw them onto the fire. The fire flickered and then flared up before her.

She was about to say her name when the fire started crackling loudly; she felt a swirling breeze wrap itself around her. The crackling got so loud that it hurt her ears. With a surge of immense power, the fire burst up and out, flaring so high that it seemed to go right through the roof of the bower. She felt the ground shake. When she looked down, she saw that the ground was dissolving beneath her feet. Looking back up at the fire, she saw a small whirlwind forming just over the logs. The swirling fire grew larger and stronger; Ella felt she would have to look away or be sick. Suddenly, a huge beam of concentrated light shot out directly at her. She felt an intense burst of energy hit the front of her body; with a small, bright flash, that energy entered her body. The intensity of it was so great it brought her to her knees.

She was sure she could hear Story Teller screaming. It sounded like she was screaming her name, but the words sounded as if they were coming from far, far away. Ella tried to turn and look at Story Teller, but she could not make her head turn or any other part of her body move. The air around her began to frizzle and snap. Everything around her—the bower, the grass, even the stones of the fire pit—was gone, enveloped in a supercharged vapor.

It's funny what you think of in times of great stress and fear. At that moment, Ella thought she'd done something wrong; she hadn't even said her name. *This is it*, she thought. *This is what it feels like when a fairy dies, and I won't be able to say goodbye to my parents.* Her heart pounded against her ribs, and her head started to feel fuzzy. Warmth traveled throughout her body and intensified.

Unable to move or speak, she watched the fire. The flame started to flicker, as though a million lightning bugs had flown into it, and the entire fire lit up with an array of amazingly beautiful colors. She was sure there were even a few colors she hadn't seen before. The colors started to flicker faster and faster, making her even dizzier. The air around her was so charged with energy that it was becoming increasingly difficult to breathe. When she looked around, she saw a lot of nothingness! She seemed to be floating, but her wings were still tucked in and closed. Complete darkness surrounded her, with a swirling mist of pure energy hovering everywhere. The only things she could still see were the fire and its colors, although the fire looked like it was coming out of a deep black void.

Then she heard the voice. It came from inside her and felt like it was part of her. It wasn't loud, but it sounded extremely deep, and she could feel each word vibrate inside her head.

"Ella, Princess of the Blue Wings, descendent of Eamon, King of the Blue Wings. Hear my words." The voice paused. The swirling energy continued intensifying. Ella's wings emerged and spread open, and she saw a brilliant light from the corner of her eye as her wings began to glow. She was willing to bet they were glowing even brighter than the fire as she felt power coursing through them.

"Princess Ella, you hold within all gifts given to you by your ancestors! These abilities and powers will manifest when you have need of them. Show great care with whom you choose to share these powers, as they may be used against you. It is your destiny to ensure the continuance of the Blue Wings' bloodline and be a leader to your people. When you reach your thirty-fifth year, the aging process will end. A queen must look young enough to handle all, yet old enough to have the needed knowledge. A life mate is imminent, and several will come forward in time. It will be with their help that you will pass on the Blue Wings' bloodline.

Traveling will be mandatory, as you must return home. You need to ensure the safety of your kind."

The words vibrated throughout Ella's body. She felt them so strongly that she knew she would never forget them. All she could think of were two questions: How would she know where she would find safety? And how was she to find the other Blue Wings? Ella hadn't spoken her questions out loud, but the voice began to answer.

"Go home, Ella, Princess of the Blue Wings! Go back to where it all began! It is there that you will find your answers. When you find yourself, you will find safety for you and the others. Go home, and your people will come to you. All will know when it is time.

"Be strong, Princess Ella, and be watchful. Take great care when choosing those who are close to you. A time will come when whom you believed to be a friend will turn out to be your enemy! You now hold four close to your heart. They are the ones to depend on and put your trust in. It is your guardian who has the greatest strength. He has much knowledge, so look to him for your greatest support and rely on his wisdom to help guide you. The two of you are now deeply connected.

"Further answers will be found in what has come to you from the past. When looked upon, it can show you your destined path and help find lost connections. Trust in yourself and your abilities; you are much stronger than you believe. Open your eyes to see what isn't, in order to find what is!"

As the last of the words vibrated through her body, everything went dark. *Wait!* Ella thought. *What does that mean? I don't understand.* The darkness pulled at the edges of her mind. She couldn't keep her eyes open, and all the sounds around her started to become muted and faint. She couldn't fight it even if she wanted to; she was becoming part of what was around her. She felt herself falling, and she just let herself go.

Chapter 14

It was difficult to take a breath. Everything hurt, even her wings. All she wanted to do was go back into the quiet, peaceful darkness; but the darkness was slipping away. She was able to see some light behind her eyelids. Was someone calling her name? Yes, she could hear her name being called again and again, and there was more than one voice. *Oh, please,* she thought, *just go away and leave me alone.* They didn't, of course; they were still calling her! At first they sounded very far away, but their voices were getting closer and closer. Who could be calling for her?

"Ella, are you all right? Can you hear me? I think she's coming around."

Ella felt something wet and slimy roll across her face. Slowly she opened her eyes, only to see Brogan's large head right over the top of hers. His paws were on her chest. *Ah,* she thought, *that's why it was so hard to take a breath.* Suddenly it hit her; she knew what the wet, slimy thing was.

"Brogan, did you just lick my face?" She said this with as much disgust in her voice as she could manage, but the words came out kind of croaky and weak. Considering that he was practically standing on her chest, she thought she had done rather well.

Brogan's eyes widened, and he gave a gravely growl. "Princess, you're all right?"

Ella hadn't noticed it at first, but when she looked into his eyes, she could see real fear. That shook her up a little.

"I would be better if you'd get off of me." She had tried to keep her voice even and soft to take the sting out of her words, but it was still difficult to speak with him standing on her.

"Ella, oh my, you gave us such a scare!" Ella's mother was standing right behind Brogan. For the first time, Ella noticed that both her parents were crying. What was going on?

"What happened? What are you talking about?" Ella looked around and realized they were at the village bower. The memory of what happened crashed down on her. Ella looked around the room for Story Teller. She was standing on the other side of her parents. She looked older and very, very pale.

Brogan lifted his front paws off of her chest and bent his head down, clamping the front of her dress in his teeth. He slowly pulled, giving Ella no choice but to sit up. Once she was sitting, she noticed that her body was still vibrating. Her parents took her arms and helped her onto her feet.

"Brogan, you ever lick my face again, I'm going to shave your head bald while you sleep!" It was the first thing that came to mind.

Ella wiped the slobber off her chin and cheek. When she looked over at Brogan, he let out a small chuckle.

"I'm not kidding, Brogan. That was just disgusting. Also, you may want to consider eating some wild mint leaves; you have the very worst breath!"

Brogan gave Ella a dirty look. "I'm not a rabbit, little one. I don't eat leaves!" He rolled his eyes.

"You will have to excuse Ella, Brogan. When she was small, a frog jumped onto her cheek. Ever since, she cannot stand to have anything wet or slimy touch her face." Ella's mother gave Ella a warning look.

"Why are all of you in here?" Ella looked at her parents and Brogan. "I thought you had to stay outside for my ceremony."

Everyone stopped their fussing and turned shocked faces to Ella. Story Teller spoke first. "Ella, don't you know what happened? I have never, in all my years—and that's more than I want to admit—seen anything like what happened here today." Story Teller's voice was shaking. "Ella, you need to tell me what you remember."

Ella was stunned. "Didn't you see what happened? Couldn't you hear the words of the fire?"

Ella knew that during other fairies' fire ceremonies, Story Teller was present. This was essential and part of her responsibility to each fairy who came of age. Also, she was the only one who had the power of the village fire. Without her, the fire would not speak. It was her duty to document all information that was passed on to each new full-fledged fairy. Keeping records of what had occurred during each ceremony was extremely important for future reference.

"I could barely see you, Ella, and no words were said that I could hear. I have never seen the fire do what it did today." Story Teller spoke quickly. She stopped and blew out a large breath. "Ella, you were taken into the fire! The flames of the fire burst up and went through the roof of the bower."

Everyone looked up at the roof. Ella could see a perfect circle of scorched wood, with small holes randomly scattered throughout, where the fire had burned right through.

Story Teller waited until everyone's eyes were back on her before she continued speaking. "The fire flowed out so far that it was no longer contained within its pit. When it came out of the pit, it pulled you inside, and you were taken to the center. You were floating in the middle, in a kind of kneeling position. Your wings were open, glowing even brighter than the fire!" Story Teller cleared her throat. "The heat from the flames was so great that I was unable to get close. I believed you would be burned alive! The sound of it was deafening. It was incredible; it sounded like several thunder claps all happening at the exact same time. I have never witnessed such an event, nor have I ever heard a tale of something like this happening in the past."

"We came in when we heard Story Teller screaming your name. We could see the flames shooting out, and we knew something was wrong," Ella's father said quietly.

Story Teller came closer. "Ella, first, are you hurt in any way?"

Ella shook her head. "I'm a little sore, but otherwise I'm fine"

"Then can you tell us what happened?"

Chapter 15

Ella told them what happened, everything she could remember, which she was sure was every moment. It felt like it had been burned into her memory.

"I understood everything that was said up until the last few parts. Some things were said that I'm not really sure about." Ella closed her eyes as she repeated what had been told to her: "'Go back to where it all began! It is there that you will find your answers. When you find yourself, you will find safety for you and the others. Go home, and your people will come to you.'" Ella opened her eyes and looked at Story Teller. "What do you think that means? What does it mean, 'where it all began' and 'go home'? Does it mean our tree hut?"

Story Teller shook her head. No one else said anything.

"Well, how about this part." Ella quoted more of the voice's words. "'A time will come when whom you believed to be a friend will turn out to be your enemy.' Who is my enemy? It can't be one of you, because the fire clearly stated that you are the ones I can trust."

"I think that part means you shouldn't always think that just because someone is being nice to you that they're a friend," Story Teller said quietly.

"Maybe, but I don't get the feeling that was how it was meant. Here's the part I'm really having a hard time with, because it makes no sense to me." Ella took a deep breath and closed her eyes again. "'Further answers will be found in what has come to you from the past. When looked upon, it can show you your destined path and help find lost connections. Open your eyes to see what isn't, in order to find what is.' What can that mean?" Ella opened her eyes and waited. She was expecting Story Teller to say something, but, to her surprise, it was Brogan who spoke.

"I'm not sure of the very last part, but I think I know what it's referring to when it speaks of something from the past. Ella, I gave you something that came from the past." Brogan willed Ella to make the connection. She reached up and grabbed the amulet.

"My amulet." Her voice was low and breathy. "Of course!"

"How will the amulet help you?" Her mother looked confused.

"I'm not really sure how, but it's definitely what the fire was referring to. When I was taken into the fire, my chest started to get very warm. It must have been the amulet's power. I thought at the time that it was the heat of the fire, but that really doesn't make any sense, because I would have felt the heat on the rest of my body."

"Perhaps the last part of the message, 'Open your eyes to see what isn't, in order to find what is,' has something to do with the amulet as well." Ella's father looked at his daughter. She could see the strain reflected in the depths of his eyes.

"I'm not sure, but it would make sense if it did." Ella smiled at her father, trying to reassure him.

"This ceremony is not yet over. In all the confusion, I almost forgot about the ceremony loaf. It must be eaten." Story Teller gestured toward the back of the bower. "Please, everyone, come to the back with me."

They all followed Story Teller to the back, where a table was set. The ceremonial loaf waited on a platter in the middle. Next to it was a wooden pitcher containing the ceremonial wine.

"Oh, my, the loaf seems much larger than I remember. How are we going to eat it all?" Ella's mother looked at her husband as she said this.

"Story Teller, are you allowed to partake in the loaf with us? You are, after all, part of this family!" Ella's father smiled.

"I'm unable to help you. As the keeper of the fire, it is my duty to ensure that all things are done properly, but I cannot be part of the ceremony itself."

Ella looked at Brogan. "Brogan will help us eat the loaf. He's part of this family now, and I dare anyone to say otherwise!"

Story Teller gave it some thought and then nodded. "Yes, Brogan is considered family. He'll be allowed to help you eat the ceremonial loaf. The only stipulation is that he'll be required to sit at the table with you."

Ella heard Brogan mutter, "Won't *this* be interesting." He looked at Ella and then carefully pulled out a chair by hooking it with his large muzzle. Once he had the chair out far enough, he came around to the side, lifted his two front paws onto the edge of the table, and slid his back end onto the seat of the chair. Just before he was fully on, he gave a small little whine.

"Ella, I need you to pull my tail out for me." Brogan said this as quietly as he could. Ella knew how hard it must be for the warrior wolf to ask for help, and it deeply moved her that he would go through all this for her. She didn't think Brogan had ever sat in a chair like this. Why would he have? He was a wolf.

Ella pulled Brogan's tail free. "Thank you, Brogan, for doing this for me."

Brogan mumbled something and turned his head. Ella was surprised he would be embarrassed by her words.

Story Teller sliced the ceremonial loaf. The largest piece she handed to Brogan. She poured the wine into three clay goblets and gave them to Ella and her parents. Brogan declined the wine.

After all the loaf had been consumed, Story Teller kissed Ella on the forehead. "Your ceremony is finished, little one. I wish you luck for the future."

Each of Ella's parents hugged Ella. Ella was extremely glad the fire ceremony was over and done with! This was just the beginning, though. Things were about to get a lot more intense.

Chapter 16

She knew someone was coming; she'd heard footsteps a while ago. No one else would have heard them, but she'd been expecting a visit tonight and was listening for them.

When the bush rustled, she didn't bother turning around. She already knew who it was.

"Well, what news do you bring me tonight?"

"It is done. The Blue Wing princess had hers fire ceremony this morning, and, as yous suspected, it was nothing like any other ceremony ever given. Even the Keeper of the Fires was unprepared for what happened."

This information didn't surprise her. She'd seen it in a vision. "Was all of the ceremonial loaf consumed?"

"Yes. The wolfs was invited to the table. Hes helped to ensure all was eaten. That had been somewhat of a surprise to mes. Hes didn't have any of the wine, though. I'ms not sure if that will make a difference or not."

"The wolf is family now. He was meant to help eat the loaf. His not having any wine won't affect the outcome. Did the young fairy understand all that was told to her?"

"Is wasn't able to get close enough to hears all of what was said, but Is don't believe so. There were several things that shes was puzzling out with those who were with hers. Is do know shes has some knowledge of the amulet, and that will help hers in some ways."

"Good; that's a start. The rest will come in time. She has much to learn yet. Was there any talk of her traveling soon?"

"No. Only what was said by the fires."

"It will have to happen soon. Were any other fairies there besides her family?"

"No. Is looked."

"Good. It would have done her no good to have others witness what transpired." She paused for a moment. Now that it was all happening, there were so many things to consider.

"She and the wolf will have to travel soon. She must find the answers. I want you to go back and watch over them. As I've said before, make sure your presence goes unnoticed. My magic is strong, but there is still the chance someone will see past it. It would do us no good if they discovered they were being watched. Brogan is a warrior, trained to sense things out of the ordinary. Don't take his abilities for granted. You'll need to be more careful now than ever. He'll be on high alert now that she's become a full-fledged fairy. Come back and report to me after seven nights have passed. Do you understand?"

"Yes, Is understand. Will yous be going forward soon, as planned?"

"The wheels have already been set in motion. It won't be long now. Have a care for your safety, my good friend. We shall talk soon."

She looked up to the stars and the moon as she listened to his footsteps fade. She wasn't sure what was going to happen now; in her visions, she wasn't able to see past Ella's fire ceremony. All she knew for sure was that she wasn't going to allow what had happened in the past to happen again! That was something she could at least act on. She prayed all would be well.

Chapter 17

It was a beautiful, clear sunny day. Brogan was lying in the shade of a tree, watching Ella as she visited with her so-called friend Astral. Ella had asked him to sit a little farther away so she and her friend could talk. Brogan wasn't happy about this; he didn't like or trust Astral. He knew that fairy was up to no good, and he couldn't understand why Ella didn't see that.

As he lay there, he kept watch. Ella was much taller than the rest of her clan. She had flawless skin, as do all fairies, but hers seemed to glow. He thought Ella was much prettier than the other young fairies her age. Astral, especially, seemed plain next to Ella. Astral had the usual light-blond hair and brown eyes. Perhaps her face was pleasing to look at, but in no way was she as pretty as Ella. It was sad to know Ella was being shunned by her own people; she was so self-conscious now she wouldn't even fly anywhere, fearful that someone should see her blue wings.

Brogan gave himself a mental shake. It was interesting how attached he'd become to Ella in such a short period of time. He'd only heard about the connection that grew between guardian and guarded; it meant they were destined to be together. It was one thing to hear about it but quite another to have it happen. He knew they would be connected for all time now and that nothing could break that connection except death. Never before had something so profoundly moved him, and he knew that if something were to happen to Ella, he would be affected far more then he'd like.

Big changes were coming, but what those changes were, he didn't know. He could only hope Ella would find her abilities soon and that the two of them would get through it all.

Ella and Astral sat on the edge of a small clearing, enjoying the feel of the sun on their skin and wings. Ella didn't often let her wings be seen, but today only a small group of fairy children from their clan were there to see them. She and Astral watched these younger fairies play around and try to do tricks in the air when they were flying. The kids flew past one another at breakneck speeds, trying to outdo one another with aerial acrobatics. They did swirls, swoops, flips, and dives. Some even played chicken in the air. They would fly at each other as fast as they could until one of them swerved away at the last moment. Others tried to see who could fly the highest. A group of young girls made small pyramids high in the sky, while others did flips and summersaults. As Ella watched, one of the small boys almost hit a tree while trying a swirl and swoop. Her heart pounding, she looked away.

Astral noticed that Ella's attention was back on her. "Well, tell me about your fire ceremony! What did the fire tell you?" Astral's beautiful face looked to Ella, demanding answers.

Ella leaned onto her hands and let her head fall back so she could feel the sun on her face. "Let's see. First I was told that I hold the abilities of my ancestors. I'll stop aging at thirty-five. I will someday meet several possible life mates. I will have to travel; this cannot be where I live out all my days. I think that sums up everything. Oh, and Brogan is considered my family, so he was allowed to help eat the ceremonial loaf."

"I'm not sure why you want a wolf being considered your family. He probably dropped fleas all over your loaf."

"Astral, don't be like that. You know why he's here and why he must be with me at all times."

Ella looked at Brogan, lying in the shade of a large tree, looking like he was having a nice afternoon nap. Ella knew better. He wasn't sleeping; he was on high alert for any problems or uninvited guests. They had already had a fight this morning when Ella asked him to sit farther away from her and Astral. He really didn't like being that far away from her, because if something were to happen, he might not be able to get to her fast enough. Plus, he made it very clear that he didn't like or trust Astral. Apparently, Astral didn't like him that much, either.

"All I'm saying is, no way would I share my bread with a wolf. Especially that wolf." Astral sent the evil eye in Brogan's direction. "Anyway, I'm very upset with you, Ella! I thought for sure you would have come and told me all about your ceremony. Didn't I tell you all about mine later on that evening? Didn't I share every little detail with you? And do you want to know why? Because you're my best friend, and that's what best friends do—they share everything." Astral took a deep breath. "I waited for you last night, expecting you to come over and tell me all about it, and you didn't bother to show up. I could have been out with Char, but I was willing to put you before him! So you better have a good reason for not coming over, because I had to spend the evening listening to my mother complain!"

Ella was more than used to Astral's rambling. Astral loved to talk, so Ella always just let her. "After my ceremony was over, we all flew up to Little Lost Lake. We spent a quiet day there, and it was really nice."

Ella's parents had wanted to go somewhere that would ensure some peace after all Ella had gone through that morning. Brogan followed them from below.

"Mother and I picked flowers and a few herbs, and we all went for a swim in the lake. We didn't get back until late. Sorry, Astral, but that's why I didn't come to see you. That, and I didn't want to deal with your mother."

The truth was, her parents didn't want her telling anyone anything about what had happened that morning. She knew she couldn't hide all of it, and she also knew Astral would ask questions. How could Ella ignore her? Ella, her parents, and Brogan spent much of the night formulating what they would tell others if anyone were to ask. They knew the roof of the village bower was something they couldn't hide. Others were sure to ask questions. Suddenly the roof was scorched and full of holes, right after Ella's ceremony—no, that was not something they could hide. It required an explanation.

"You said you were going to have your ancestors' abilities? This means you'll have more than one? What are your abilities, then?"

"I'm not really sure; it wasn't explained. All the fire said was that I would have my ancestors' abilities. Nothing else was clear."

Astral made a *humph* sound. "Well, what ancestors was the fire referring to?"

"I'm not sure. I told you, it wasn't made really clear." Ella hated to lie to Astral, but she knew if she told her friend too much, the rest of the village would know about it by the end of the next day. Ella loved her friend very much, but Astral couldn't keep a secret if her life depended on it. She just loved to talk too much, something she'd inherited from her mother.

"Ella, do you know everyone is talking about the roof of the village bower? It wasn't like that before your ceremony, and then you go in, and there are holes all over the place!"

"Astral, the holes are not all over the place. They're just over the fire pit. Story Teller gave me the herbs to put into the fire, and when the fire blazed up, it went a little higher than anyone expected. Story Teller wasn't sure why it happened but thought maybe she might have put too much of something in the mix of herbs. Anyway, my father is there now, helping to fix it."

"Are you sure that's what really happened?"

"As far as I know, that's what happened, and I was there. Besides, what else could it be?" Ella felt another twinge of guilt, but Brogan would kill her if she told Astral the truth. Knowing this made it easier to tell Astral what they'd agreed on.

Astral looked at Ella for a moment. She must have decided to let things be and move on to a new topic. "Wow! You have to age all the way to thirty-five? And here I was upset about twenty-nine. Thirty-five is positively ancient! You're going to have wrinkles and maybe even gray hair. You poor, poor thing!"

Ella knew Astral wasn't feeling that sorry for her; she was just glad it was Ella aging that long and not her. "Well, thirty-five is a little older than I'd hoped for, but what can I do? It's not like I can change it."

"Wait a minute. You said you have to move? As in, move away from this village? You want to move away from me?" Tears swelled in Astral's eyes. "You can't move away from me. We've been friends for way too long. You really want to move away from here and leave everything you know? What about your parents?"

"Astral, stop! Gee, of course I don't want to move. It was something the fire said. There will come a time when I will leave here to go elsewhere. It didn't mention when or where. I'm not going to spend a lot of time worrying about it until the time comes. I'm hoping it won't be for a long while. Besides, if I leave, then there is the potential of meeting my possible life mate, which, I can tell you right now, I'm not ready for. I have enough problems in my life without adding to them." Ella rolled her eyes. Both girls giggled. "Speaking of life mates, how are things going with your three potentials?"

Ella knew how to steer the conversation to safer topics. As usual, Astral was more than happy to discuss herself and talk to Ella about her many problems.

Some time passed with the girls sitting and talking. Ella was intently listening to her friend when a sudden jolt rushed through her mind. She started to envision something moving through the trees behind them and knew that whatever it was, it was still some distance away. With the speed at which it traveled, though, it wouldn't take long to reach them.

Ella cut Astral off in mid-sentence. "Astral, listen to me. Something very large is coming toward us. I'm not sure what it is, but it is extremely large and will be here right away. I need you to take the younger ones back to the village. It's coming from behind us, so you should reach the village before it gets here. You must hurry!" Ella called to all the children.

"What are you talking about? I don't sense anything."

"Trust me; something is coming. Take the children, and we'll talk later. I need to speak with Brogan."

The children gathered around the girls. Ella challenged them to race Astral back to the village and then lined them up and counted to three. The children took off with cheers and laughter. Astral gave Ella a look.

"I promise to explain later. Thank you for taking the children." Ella hugged her friend and watched her chase the young ones.

Concerned with Astral and the children, Ella hadn't heard Brogan hurry to her side. "Ella, someone approaches. I don't want you to be seen, so make yourself invisible again and stay right by my side."

Ella allowed herself to disappear and quietly stood next to Brogan. Silently they waited; they didn't have to wait long.

Chapter 18

The hair on the back of Brogan's neck stood up, and every muscle in his body tensed. The look on his face was so fierce it scared her.

In a very hushed voice, Ella whispered to Brogan, "I had a vision earlier. I saw someone coming, but the picture was unclear. That's why I sent Astral and the children away. The vision is much clearer now, maybe because it's closer. It looks like a wolf, but he's as large as you, maybe even bigger. Wait, he's stopped!"

Suddenly a deep, growling howl pierced the quiet forest. Birds took to the air, and small ground animals scurried away. Ella had never heard anything like it. Brogan visibly relaxed.

"I know who it is—a warrior from my clan." Brogan looked around uncertainly. "Ella, I want you to stay here while I go meet him. I'm sure everyone heard him, but I'd rather he remain unseen. It's for our safety as well as his."

Brogan let out a howl in reply. Ella had thought the first howl was loud, but it was nothing compared to Brogan's. She wasn't sure if she'd ever hear properly again.

"Maybe you could warn me the next time you howl like that! At least let me cover my ears." Ella shook her head, trying to stop the ringing in her ears.

"Make sure you remain unseen while I speak to my clansman. You're not safe alone."

Ella found a place to stand under one of the large trees surrounding the clearing. She'd just reached the tree when a small mouse ran into her leg, so hard that he knocked himself onto his side. He was obviously dazed; when he tried to stand, he staggered and then fell back down. *Poor little thing*, she thought. She should have been paying more attention. She would have to keep a closer watch for the creatures around her, at least until Brogan came back. When she crouched to check on the mouse, a bird swooped down, narrowly missing her head.

Wow, that was close, she thought. *Maybe being invisible isn't such a good thing!* She looked down at the mouse as he attempted to get up again.

"Sorry, little mouse. I didn't mean to hurt you." She said this as quietly as possible while scanning the area for more unexpected wildlife. She really hadn't been expecting an answer.

"It's all right. I should have been watching. Wait a minute— who said that?" The little mouse shook his head firmly. "Maybe I hit my head harder than I thought." His squeaky voice paused for a moment as he looked around. "No, not the hit! I knew I shouldn't have eaten that old cheese! Who knows how long it was there." The mouse sat up, cleaned off his whiskers with his two front paws, and then scampered into the forest.

Ella sat down, leaning against the tree. *That mouse could hear me, and I could hear him!* She struggled to wrap her mind around what had just happened. No one she knew could speak to or understand small animals. The bigger animals, yes; many of her kind had that ability. The smaller ones were different for some reason. Maybe it was their size, which made their voices too quiet for any fairy to hear. She wasn't really sure of the reason, but she was sure she'd just heard that mouse. As she contemplated this discovery, a large snake slithered down from one of the branches above her.

"Isss can tassst you, but Isss cant sssee you." The snake's tongue flicked in and out of its mouth, tasting the air.

Ella looked up to see the snake hanging just over her head. This was turning out to be quite the eventful day! "I'm sorry to disappoint you, but I'm much too big to be your meal. You'll have to look elsewhere, my friend."

"Whossss there? What kindsss of sssstrange magicsss issss thissss?" The snake slowly recoiled.

"I wish I could answer that for you. I'm not even sure I understand it myself."

The snake slithered back up. Considering all that had happened to her over the last few days, she didn't know why she should think this was any stranger than anything else!

A little time passed before she heard and felt Brogan walking back. She waited until she could see him before she stood up.

"It's only me, small one. You can reappear now. My clansman has left."

Ella wished herself to be seen again and then joined Brogan.

"How did you know I was near?"

Brogan began to walk back toward the village. "I can smell you, of course!"

"Why did your clansman come?"

"He came to deliver a message. We will discuss what was said when we get back to the village." He made sure Ella was following. "The message should be heard with your parents present. There's no point explaining it twice. Perhaps we should get Story Teller on our way through. I believe she should hear the message, too."

Ella took large steps to keep up with him. "I'm not sure where Story Teller will be, but we can check the village bower. If she isn't there, we can look in her tree hut." Ella tried very hard not to seem overly anxious, but worry had settled within her, and she couldn't shake the feeling that another upheaval was on its way. "Is the message bad? Do you have to leave for another assignment? Something has happened and you have to go back home?"

"Nothing like that. I am to be with you for many more years, little one." Brogan slowed down and waited until Ella caught up. He brushed his head against Ella's hand in reassurance. "Wait until we get everyone together, and I will explain everything. I don't think the message is bad, but I'm sure you won't like it very much."

Ella closed her eyes for a moment and then continued to follow Brogan. It wouldn't do any good to ask about it further. It sure didn't sound like it was going to be something she really wanted to hear, anyway.

She had no idea how right she was!

Chapter 19

It took them a while to find Story Teller; she wasn't at the village bower or at home. She was visiting one of the village elders, and by the time they found out where she was, she was on her way home again.

When they reached Ella's tree hut, Ella was disappointed to find that her mother had left to attend to a sick neighbor. She was ready to crawl out of her skin as she waited to hear the message. Her mother took forever to get home. Eventually they were all together, sitting around a large oval table. Everyone turned to Brogan, who stood beside the small fireplace in the kitchen.

"A message was sent to our clan. A witch has requested that Ella come before her. She wishes to have a meeting. The witch says she has some information for Ella that she believes will be of great help." Brogan paced. He didn't have much room; he could take only two or three steps in either direction.

"It's not known what this information is or how it might be helpful. Our clan has known of this witch for many centuries, but no one knows very much about her. She has kept to herself over the years, and any stories about her have long been forgotten. The head of our clan, the oldest of all warrior wolves, knows her from a time that is almost forgotten. He has indicated she is a friend, not a threat to us." Brogan sat down in front of the fire. "I myself met her once, but that was a long time ago. I didn't get a bad feeling from her then.

"Though no one knows very much about her, we do know she was one of the first witches to come to this world. She and her sister arrived shortly after the first Silver Wings. Therefore, she is very old and has more powers than any other witch we know of."

Brogan looked at Ella. "I think it's important for you to know that her sister was the witch from whom the Silver Wings gained the magic to destroy the Blue Wings. When her sister found out what her magic had been used for, she became unbalanced. It's said she was so consumed with guilt over the destruction of the Blue Wings that she couldn't bear to live and took her own life."

There was a moment of silence as everyone let this information sink in. Story Teller spoke first.

"Brogan, would you happen to know the name of the witch who has summoned Ella? Perhaps I've heard of her."

"Her name is Hettie, and her sister's name was Mari."

"Yes, I've heard of her. I have also heard the story of her sister taking her own life but not the reason for her doing so. I've heard that the immense grief over losing her sister is why Hettie cut all ties to the outside world. She placed a spell around herself and her dwelling, allowing no one to come near her. The things I have heard about her haven't been all that good. She's known to be a little eccentric and unbalanced herself. She also happens to be the oldest witch anyone has ever known to exist."

"I know Ella is of age now and can make her own decisions, but, as her mother, I would like to voice my opinion. I don't know why this witch has requested to see Ella, but I honestly don't think it would be wise to go. Brogan would be no match against powerful witchcraft, and Ella doesn't know what her abilities are yet. This could be a trick. We just don't know!"

Ella's father stood behind his wife, placing his hands on her shoulders. "We have to remember that she is a very powerful witch. Let's say we don't listen and ignore her summons. What happens then? If you ask me, that would be asking for trouble." He paused for a moment and closed his eyes. "Story Teller, have you heard of anyone actually coming to harm from this witch? Has she hurt anyone you know of?"

Story Teller thought for a moment. "I don't think so, but I can't really be sure. I'm not even sure if the stories I've heard were based on truth, fear, or rumor."

Ella's father continued, "Brogan said she means us no harm. I think it might be in Ella's best interest to go and hear what this witch has to say."

Ella could see the strain on her father's face. He sounded extremely tired, and she knew these words weren't easy for him to say.

Brogan started his pacing again. "I don't believe there's any reason for us to fear her. If there was cause for concern, it would have been passed on in the message from my clan." Brogan stopped pacing and looked at everyone. "Frankly, meeting the witch it not what concerns me; it's the traveling to get to her that worries me. It'll be a full day's travel just to reach the meeting place. There's no way of knowing if we'll encounter trouble on the way there or back."

"If this meeting is to happen, I think it would be best if we come with you." Ella's father looked at Brogan.

"That wouldn't be wise. It'll be difficult enough for me to protect Ella. Plus, the more we have in our group, the easier it will be to detect us. If we go, we must go alone. It'll be safer for Ella."

Ella had had enough! They were all speaking as though she wasn't even there. Worse, they were acting like she was a small fairy, unable to decide for herself! "Would anyone care to hear what I might have to say about all this? It's about me, after all!" Shocked, everyone turned to Ella. She'd tried and failed to keep the anger from her voice. She took a big breath and let it out slowly. Now that she had their attention, she would try to speak more calmly.

"The risks involved in getting there matter not. I must go see her. Don't ask me how I know this, but it's of the utmost importance that I do. I'm meant to hear what she has to say."

Her mother's mouth opened, but Ella lifted her hand. "I believe this witch means me no harm and will, in fact, greatly help me gain some understanding." Again she saw her mother start to object, so she lifted her hand up as a warning and continued to speak. "As I said, I'm not sure how I can be so sure, but I am, and I feel this very strongly! I'm sorry if this sounds rude, but it doesn't matter what any of you think or say. This is up to me to decide, and I've decided I must go. Father, I understand your reasons for wanting to come, but I also know you can't. As Brogan pointed out, it will only increase the dangers."

Ella looked at her parents, willing them to understand. She could tell neither one was happy with her decision, but that couldn't be helped. Silence was all she got in response.

"Brogan, when are we to see this witch?"

"We must leave after five days have passed. The morning of the sixth day, we leave at dawn."

"Then it's settled. That's when we leave."

Ella walked onto the veranda and leaned against the rail. She wasn't happy she'd talked to her parents that way, but her decision felt right. She knew the next five days would be the longest five days of her life. Her mother would take every opportunity to bombard her with well-meant protests and guilt-inducing tears. Perhaps she should remain invisible for the next five days. Her mother couldn't smell her the way Brogan could.

Brogan watched his young charge through the door. He was greatly impressed with how Ella handled that. She was beginning to show great strength. He knew she would need this strength to handle what awaited her.

Chapter 20

Astral flew up to her veranda and quietly walked into the tree hut. If she could avoid her mother for only a few hours, then perhaps she could come up with something better to tell her. Hopefully it would get her mother off her back for a while.

"Astral, you wouldn't be trying to sneak past me, would you?" Asia stood outside the door.

"Mother, you startled me! Of course I wasn't sneaking. I wasn't sure if the baby was sleeping or not. You know what she's like when she gets woken up early." They both knew Astral was lying.

"Well, are you going to tell me or not? What did that good-for-nothing, blue-winged freak have to say?"

Astral really wanted to point out that before Ella's wings turned blue, her mother had wished Ella was her daughter instead of Astral. She said nothing only because she liked living more than she liked making jabs at her mother.

"Ella said it was Story Teller's herbs that made the fire burn the roof."

"That's the best they could come up with? You'd think they could lie better than that!" Asia snorted. "What about her ceremony? What was she told?"

"She said she was destined to move but wouldn't right away. She is to meet several possible matches. She will have her ancestors' abilities, and she will stop aging at thirty-five."

"She's going to stop breathing long before she reaches thirty-five. What are her ancestors' abilities?"

"She says she doesn't know what they are, only that there will be more than one." Astral lowered her head. She knew where this was going, and her mother didn't disappoint her.

"More than one!" Asia's voice rose a couple of octaves. "She's to have several abilities, and you get one very useless ability. Again, I question why I have to have such a useless daughter." Regaining control of her temper, Asia added, "I suppose it won't matter what abilities that blue-winged freak possesses, because she can't use them if she's dead, now can she?"

Astral looked up when her mother went silent. Asia took several steps closer to her, hate reflected in her eyes. "I'm going to assume that you didn't succeed in taking care of her today. Am I right?" Asia snarled.

"I couldn't. The wolf was there the whole time. Plus, there were too many young fairies around."

"You could have arranged something, you useless little twit! How many more chances do you think you're going to have? You need to get this done before she gets her abilities or before she moves away." Asia shoved Astral hard as she walked past her. "You'd better not continue to disappoint me, young fairy! Otherwise, that blue-winged freak won't be the only one to have a shortened life span!"

Astral watched her mother disappear into the heart of the tree hut. As quickly as she could, she ran upstairs before her mother could come back to rant at her some more. After locking herself in her room, she collapsed on her bed and finally allowed the tears to flow.

How would she do this terrible thing to Ella? The problem was, she didn't hate Ella. Who cared if her wings were blue? Her mother cared, that was who. As long as her mother was alive,

Astral had no choice but to do as she was told. Perhaps if she took care of Ella, her mother would finally love her. Well, maybe *love* was pushing it. She didn't think her mother was actually capable of loving others. If not love, then perhaps a little pride in her daughter, a little respect?

Astral pictured her friend's face. Maybe there was a small part of her that hated Ella. After all, Ella had everything. Her parents adored her, and everyone used to think she could do no wrong, even her own mother. Now she was some kind of princess? That was just wrong!

Astral let her jealousy take over, and she embraced her resentment. Perhaps taking care of Ella wouldn't be as hard as she'd thought!

Chapter 21

Ella and Brogan went to the village bower to see Story Teller. Story Teller kept maps of the middle world, and Ella wanted to see if there was a shorter way of getting to the witch's meeting point. When they arrived at the bower, they found Story Teller entertaining some fairies from a different clan.

"I think we should come back later when Story Teller is free." Ella could see some of the visitors pointing at her and whispering. It was making her very uncomfortable.

Brogan saw what was bothering Ella. "You must face your fears, little one. It'll do you no good to run away every time something makes you feel unsure."

"You don't understand, Brogan," Ella whispered. "Something weird is going on. I can hear their thoughts! And they're not good. They know I'm the blue-winged fairy because you're with me, and they want to hurt me. They are asking Story Teller about me right now."

Brogan looked at the group of fairies and growled. "Then perhaps it would be best if we came back later. I'm sure Story Teller is dealing with the matter, but we shouldn't risk it."

They quietly left the bower and started to walk back home. Ella was a very upset about what just happened. Had she really been able to hear their thoughts, or had she imagined it? She was thinking about the implications when Brogan interrupted her thoughts.

"Your abilities are beginning to make themselves known. This is just the start, so you'd better prepare yourself, Ella."

"What a terrible gift. I'd rather not hear what others think."

"I'm sorry your fist experience had to be negative. I'm sure you would feel differently if their thoughts had been more positive."

"Some things should remain private, and one's thoughts are at the top of that list." Ella kicked a stone off the path.

"At least you'll always know where you stand with strangers. You'll never have to guess what they're thinking." Brogan nudged Ella gently.

"So I'll be able to hear everyone's thoughts?" This possibility horrified Ella.

"My understanding is, you won't be able to hear the thoughts of those closest to you, like your parents, Story Teller, or me. Also, in time, you'll have control over whose thoughts you hear."

Ella stopped. "What other abilities can I look forward to suddenly popping up?"

Brogan shuffled uneasily; this conversation wasn't one he wanted to have right in the middle of the village. "I'm really not sure. I'll be able to confirm your abilities only when they begin to show. Could we discuss this when we get home? I wouldn't want others to hear."

Ella looked around. For a moment, she'd forgotten where they were. She indicated with her hand that they should continue.

They hadn't taken more than a few steps when Brogan turned, let out an ear-splitting growl, and launched himself at Ella.

Chapter 22

Brogan's front paws hit Ella's chest, pushing her back and to the side. Ella hit the ground hard, with Brogan's entire body covering her. Seconds later there was a muted thud, and bits of dirt and rock showered down on them.

Brogan's face was so close to hers that she could see every whisker on his muzzle.

"Are you all right, Princess?" His voice shook with concern.

"I think so! What in fairies' world just happened?"

"I'm not sure." When everything seemed quiet, Brogan slowly got up, pulling Ella up with him. They looked at the spot where Ella had been standing a moment before. A large rock had landed there with such force that it had created a small divot in the ground.

"That rock was meant to hit me! Someone wanted to hit me with that rock!" Ella started to shake with anger and disbelief.

Brogan growled threateningly as he surveyed the area, looking for the fairy responsible.

"This was someone from my clan. Someone who knows me threw this rock at me! I'm so sick of this." Her voice got higher as her anger took over.

Giving no thought to her action, Ella raised her right hand and pointed at the rock. A burst of energy flowed through her.

The rock whirled into the air and flew off the path with such force that when it hit a larger rock, several yards away, it exploded into tiny pieces.

Ella stumbled backward in surprise, tripped over a branch, and fell, landing on her behind. With a stunned look, she asked, "What just happened?"

Brogan almost didn't hear her because she spoke so quietly. He again helped her to her feet. He took another quick look around and nudged her to get her walking again.

"You're able to move small objects with just your thoughts. That was rather good for your first time. Let's hope whoever threw that rock didn't stick around to see that impressive show."

Ella and Brogan were almost home when a distorted voice boomed out at them. "You blue-winged freak, leave our village. You're not welcome here. Stay, and you will be sorry, you freak of nature."

Ella turned to Brogan with tears in her eyes. "I think they saw my little demonstration."

"We leave soon to meet Hettie. We'll decide later what we need to do."

The distorted voice boomed again but sounded like it was coming from a distance. "Leave our village, you freak. You'll be sorry if you don't. Both you and your pet dog! You blue-winged freak of nature."

Brogan let loose a howling growl so loud the trees around them shook. They didn't hear the voice again.

Chapter 23

Telling her parents what happened was a big mistake. They spent most of the afternoon arguing about going to meet the witch. They insisted it was too dangerous to go alone and felt they should accompany her. It was a nightmare. Brogan ended the argument by making it very clear they weren't going.

That evening, Astral came by, and the girls went to Ella's room to talk.

"Someone tried to hurt you? Well, it wouldn't be someone from our clan."

"Who else could it be?"

"You said yourself there were fairies from another village in the bower with Story Teller. It had to be one of them."

"They wouldn't have had time. It happened right after we left the bower. I would've seen one of them leaving the bower. Besides, I didn't sense a stranger close by. I know in my heart it was one of ours."

"I think you're overreacting. You were upset and wouldn't have been able to sense anything. The important thing is, you're fine. That rock didn't hit you."

"At least I'll be gone for a few days and won't have to worry about it for a while." Ella smiled thinly.

"What do you mean, you'll be gone for a few days?"

"Brogan needs to meet with one of his clansman and won't leave me here alone, especially after today. We'll be gone for only a few days."

"You're going to chase after that flea-infested, oversized dog just because he needs to talk to another flea-infested dog? Why doesn't his clansman come here?"

"That flea-infested dog saved my life today, Astral, and I would appreciate it if you would stop calling him names. Several of them are meeting, and they've chosen a central point to make it easier for all of them."

"Maybe I could go with you. You know, to keep you company while your dog is meeting with his own."

"Sorry, Astral, but we need to go alone. Brogan won't even let my parents go with us."

Astral got up. "Well, if you're going to be like that, then fine. Why you want to let a dog run your life is beyond me. Call me when you get back."

Ella watched her friend leave. *That went well*, she thought.

That night, Ella and Brogan sat under the tree hut to watch the sun set. Ella told him about her visit with Astral and the story she'd told to explain their trip.

"That was a clever story. Ella, you should be careful of this friend Astral. I don't trust her, and I don't think you should, either."

"Brogan, you don't know her like I do. We've been friends since we were small. Astral might be a little rough around the edges, but if you had a mother like hers, you would be, too."

"All I'm saying is, watch what you say around her."

"I will, I promise."

They sat quietly for a while, watching the sun go down. Just when they were about to go in, a young fairy flew by and caught her wing on a tree branch. She crashed to the ground and landed not far from their feet. Ella rushed over and helped the young fairy up. "Are you all right, honey?" she asked. She stood between the young girl and Brogan so the little fairy wouldn't be afraid.

"I think I hurt my wing." Tears started pouring down the little girl's face.

"Turn around and let me take a look. If it's bad, I can take you to see my mother. She's a healer."

The little girl turned around, and Ella saw that one of her wings had been badly torn in several spots. Placing her hands on the girl's broken wing, Ella felt heat flow from her hands to the girl. When she lifted her hands, the holes were gone, and the girl's wing was intact.

Ella turned the little fairy around and hugged her. "Your wings are fine, little one. I think you just gave yourself a scare. Now you fly home, and be very careful when you fly by trees. Next time you might not be so lucky."

The little fairy thanked Ella and flew off. Brogan gave Ella a knowing look.

"My mother's a healer, so I'm not surprised. How many more abilities do you think there are?"

"I honestly don't know. I guess we'll find out in time. It's growing late, and we need to get an early start tomorrow. It'll be a long day, and you need your rest."

"You're right. I should try to get some sleep. I'll see you bright and early tomorrow morning." Ella smiled at Brogan and left him at his spot under the tree hut.

As Ella lay in bed, a cold shiver passed over her. Something bad was going to happen tomorrow; she could feel it. She tried to think positively, but she couldn't shake the feeling of unease. It was a feeling she shouldn't have ignored.

Chapter 24

Brogan and Ella were to be on the trail just before sunrise. Ella tried to get away without waking her parents, but her mother was waiting for her at the table when she came down.

"Would it do any good to tell you once more that I don't think your going is a good idea?"

"Mother, we've been through this! I have to go. I need to hear what this witch has to say. I don't want to argue before I leave."

She hugged her mother and kissed her on the cheek. Her mother stopped her before Ella could get out the door. "Ella, hold on for a moment. I knew you would go anyway, so I thought I'd better make sure you didn't get hungry on the way. There's enough for Brogan, too." Her mother held out a basket. "You'd better make sure you come back to me, young fairy. Do you understand me?"

"Mother, I promise you, I'll be back before you even know I'm gone. Please don't cry. You're only making this harder for me. You know I have to go. I love you and I'll see you soon." Ella grabbed the basket and ran out the door. She couldn't bear to hear her mother cry.

Outside, Brogan was waiting at the bottom of the tree. She could tell by the look on his face that her mother's distress bothered him, too.

"Brogan, this is insane. We'd get there so much faster if you'd just let me fly!"

They'd been walking for a couple of hours, and it was very slow going. Brogan insisted they walk, convinced she'd be an easy target in the air. He was also concerned that he wouldn't be able to protect her if he was on the ground.

"We've already been over this! You can't fly right now." Brogan growled in frustration.

They were both on edge. It was extremely hot out; not even the shade provided relief.

"I'd like to point out that if I were not meant to fly, I wouldn't have these wings on my back. I can fly low, below the treetops, and keep my speed down so you can keep up."

"We don't have time for this." He resumed walking. "You can't fly low, because there's a good chance your wings will catch on a branch and tear; the trees here are too thick. If you got hurt, then all your energy would have to go into healing, and if you think you're tired now . . ." Brogan let that thought go, hoping she would get the message.

Ella knew he made sense, but it really irritated her. The forest they were walking through was very dense. The pine trees grew to towering heights, and the other, smaller trees and bushes closed it in even more. Their branches seemed to reach out to one another, greatly limiting the amount of free space and making their journey difficult. It was going to be the longest day ever. By the time they got to the witch, she'd be too tired to remember anything that was said.

They finally found a small game trail that cut through the forest and still took them in the right direction. It made the last few miles a little easier, but the thick underbrush still slowed their travel. It was mid-afternoon when they stopped for a bite to eat. Ella, extremely hungry, was very thankful her mother had sent the basket of food with them. She hadn't even thought of food;

she wasn't sure what they would have done if her mother hadn't been thinking.

They had just finished packing up the basket when Ella sensed other fairies nearby. "Brogan, several fairies are very close and seem to be getting closer by the minute," Ella whispered.

"I can smell them. They're getting closer," Brogan whispered back. "I don't know if they mean us harm or if it's just coincidence they're so close, but I'd rather not sick around to find out."

Quietly they entered the dense forest and started to walk away from the others. They hadn't gotten far when Ella felt a string of words enter her mind. "Be quiet or they'll hear us. I don't think they're far now." She was just about to tell Brogan when she heard another's thoughts. "I just want to blast that freak into oblivion. Those fools better be quiet or I'm going to blast them."

"Brogan, you better hurry, because I just heard some of their thoughts, and trust me, they mean us harm!"

Brogan growled. "Make yourself invisible and be as quiet as possible. Stay on the ground, because they'll expect you to fly." Brogan started back in the direction from which they'd come.

"Wait! Where are you going? If they see you, they'll hurt you, too!" For the first time, real fear rippled through her.

"Don't worry about me. I'm going to try to lead them in a different direction."

Just as Brogan turned away, a large blast erupted several feet away from them. Brogan let out a monstrous growl and turned back to Ella. A second blast exploded even closer; dirt and rock showered down. Brogan leaped on Ella, pushing her down to the ground.

Another blast ripped through the air, causing another shower of debris. Ella had just turned invisible when she saw several fairies pushing through the dense brush. Because she was touching Brogan, she knew he would disappear, too. She only hoped he'd become transparent before the fairies saw them. He was just fading out when one of the fairies spotted him.

"There's the wolf! Did you see that? Where'd he go?"

"Just throw it over there. They couldn't have gotten far."

The fairy who spoke first lifted his hand to throw something in their general direction. A deep anger filled Ella; she didn't even know who these fairies were, and they wanted to hurt her.

Brogan pulled her to her feet, but when they were both standing, she pushed him back and jammed her leg into his side; she didn't want him to become visible again. She watched the fairy across from them start to throw what was in his hand, which made her even angrier. She swung her arms up, her palms facing forward. A concentrated energy built up inside her, and she felt it suddenly release, shooting from her palms in the direction of the two fairies.

Chapter 25

There was an intense flash of bright light, and everything around them seemed to slow down. Both Ella and Brogan knew exactly when the wall of energy hit, because the small object that had been sailing toward them stopped in midair and seemed to explode in on itself. The two fairies were lifted off their feet and hurled through the air; they landed on top of each other several feet away. The vibrations of their fall actually shook the ground.

What should have taken only seconds seemed to take several minutes, but once all the energy was dispersed, time returned to normal. Brogan moved forward a little but continued to touch Ella. They waited a moment, not sure if the fairies were going to get back up; but they stayed down. She knew they were still alive, because they were groaning terribly and jerking violently on the ground. When their jerky movements subsided, they sat up, stunned looks on their faces. Slowly they tried to stand, succeeding only after several attempts. They shook their heads, trying to clear them. Ella was truly sorry it had come to this.

Brogan stepped away from her and gradually became visible. "We need to leave before their brains start working. There might be more hanging around, and I don't want to be here when they see what happened to these two."

"I think it's time for me to fly and you to do some running. There are more, and they're getting very close." Ella slumped over and felt herself flickering back to visibility. "Brogan, there's something wrong with me. Suddenly I feel extremely tired, like someone drained all my energy. And my chest is burning under my amulet."

Brogan leaped in front of Ella before she fell over. "I forgot this would happen. Using your abilities to this extent has drained you. You'll gain your strength back in time, but time isn't something we have right now. The burning you feel is the amulet trying to help you reenergize, but it'll take too long to be of any help. Ella, you'll have to climb on my back. I'll carry you. Do you think you can hang on?"

The exhaustion she felt was so extreme she hardly had the energy to speak. "I'm not sure." Her voice came out as a soft whisper. She tried to throw her leg over Brogan's back, but the effort was too much. The burning in her chest increased, and her vision blurred.

Brogan turned to help, but he was too late; Ella was already going down. Her entire body slumped over and gradually fell to the ground.

Brogan took a quick look around. The two fairies were no longer there, and an unnatural silence had settled over the forest. This couldn't be good! With his head he softly nudged Ella onto her back. Grabbing a mouthful of her dress with his teeth, he gently threw her over his head so that she was draped across his back, her head hanging down by his shoulder.

He hadn't taken more than a dozen steps before he felt Ella slowly sliding off. Before he could reach around to pull her back up, she'd slid completely off and landed on the ground in a half-seated position.

"Brogan, the burning is so bad." If he hadn't been standing so close, he probably wouldn't have heard her.

"It'll start to subside soon. Hang in there, little one." Panic set in. He was just about to get Ella back up when he heard the yelling. It was close, very close!

"Look, there they are! We got them now. Get around them."

"Those two aren't going anywhere. We have them surrounded."

"Quick, close in!"

Brogan counted ten Silver Wings, and those were only the ones he could see through the trees and brush. They all carried weapons. Knowing a battle awaited, Brogan leaped to his full height and let loose an ear-shattering war cry. He wasn't going down without a fight.

Chapter 26

The first Silver Wing ran toward Brogan, holding a large club with a sharp blade embedded in the end. With just a few steps' preparation, the fairy jumped into the air and took flight, hovering directly over Brogan. The fairy swooped down and swung the club as he approached. Brogan leaped up, grabbed the fairy by the leg with his mouth, and whipped his head to the side. The young fairy sailed through the air so fast that when he hit the tree, his club flew from his hand and he flopped to the ground, unconscious.

A scream of rage sounded, and two more fairies charged forward. Brogan waited until they were only steps away and then hurdled himself at them, he snagged one fairy by the arm with his large teeth and allowed his body weight to carry him forward. The first fairy flew back and smashed into the second. The fairies landed in a tangled heap on the ground. Brogan quickly turned and saw another fairy sneaking up on him from behind, a large knife raised in the air. Brogan charged the fairy head-on, slamming full-force into the fairy's chest. The fairy reeled, and his knife skittered into the underbrush.

Ella watched Brogan battle with fear and horror. The worst part was not being able to do anything; she still felt weak as a baby. But even if she felt strong, what could she do? She was no warrior! Tears of frustration streaked down her cheeks as she scooted to the nearest tree to get out of the way. She was almost there when two arms wrapped themselves tightly around her. She felt hot breath on her neck.

"Now it's your turn to scream, you little freak!"

Ella started to shake. It wasn't fear that caused her to tremble; it was an intense, deep-seated anger. Energy bubbled up from deep within, and renewed strength erupted. When her attacker slowly pulled her back, Ella pushed out with her arms, breaking the renegade's hold. After grabbing the nearest rock, she whirled around on her knees and bashed it into the side of the fairy's head—just as he reached down to grab her again. Blood poured from a deep gash, and the fairy fell limply to the ground.

Ella couldn't believe it! Had she just inflicted bodily harm on another living being? Even worse, what if she'd killed him? Seeing all that blood made her feel incredibly ill, and it was all she could do not to lose her lunch. She quickly pushed herself as far from her attacker as she could. She heard him make a low moan. He was alive, thank goodness—hurting, but alive.

Ella's weakness started settling back in, and her every move became more and more difficult. The worst thing she could do right now was faint, but that's what she thought might happen.

Darkness was just descending on her when she heard Brogan scream her name. She lifted her head and saw Brogan soaring over her head. She hadn't heard anyone coming up behind her, but there was a loud thud and a blood-curdling scream that was abruptly cut, leaving only silence.

In a moment, Brogan was by her side. "Ella, are you hurt?"

"No, but I'm so tired."

"I know, but we must leave. Several have run off, but it won't be long before they're back to finish the job."

"I can't even keep my head up. There's no way I can walk."

"All you have to do is get on my back and hold on. I'll do the rest."

Ella grabbed onto Brogan. But then they heard the pounding of many approaching feet.

"Ella, you need to hurry!" Brogan nudged Ella. It was too late, though. They'd run out of time. A large group of Silver Wings crashed through the trees.

Brogan pushed Ella back to the ground and turned to their attackers, preparing for a counterattack. A blinding flash of light exploded around them. The light closed in and encircled them. Brogan pushed his head against the barrier, but he was unable to move past it.

"Ella, please tell me this is your doing?"

"It wasn't me." Ella's voice was fading again.

"Well, if it wasn't you, then I think we might be in big trouble!"

Chapter 27

Brogan covered as much of Ella as he could with his body. She struggled to stay awake; she'd used too much of her energy too quickly for the first time. Shock was part of it, too. The next time she used so much energy, she would most likely recover far more quickly, but the amulet wasn't able to keep up with such an energy loss caused by first-time use.

There was a sudden zinging sound above them. Brogan barely had time to lift his head before a small round object exploded against the barrier. The explosion rebounded off the barrier, setting a few nearby trees aflame. Two more round objects zinged toward them, but they did no more damage than the first.

Brogan saw Silver Wings coming toward them. He wasn't sure who'd put the barrier up, but he wanted to be ready if the Silver Wings got through. Then he heard another strange sound, this time from inside the barrier. A sudden rush of air hit him, and it felt like his stomach had gone up into his throat. Everything around them started to spin, and Brogan heard Ella moaning loudly. As quickly as it started, it ended! With an abrupt jolt, everything returned to normal.

"Brogan, I think I'm going to be sick!" Ella did, in fact, look very green. She moaned again, turned her head, and got sick.

Brogan felt a little sick himself. When Ella was done, she wiped her mouth with her sleeve and looked up with glassy eyes.

"What just happened?"

"I'm not sure." He kept his voice low. At that moment he realized they no longer were in the forest; the barrier surrounding them was gone, too. They now sat in a large clearing filled with fragrant flowers and the hum of bees.

"I'm sorry. I had no way of warning you. But it looked like the two of you needed a little help." The new voice came from their left.

Brogan quickly covered Ella.

Someone walked out from behind a thick cropping of trees. It was difficult to get a good look at who approached, because the sun was setting and shadows covered most of that side of the clearing.

"Brogan, it's good to see you. I only wish it weren't under these circumstances!" Hettie stopped when she saw Ella. "Has she been hurt?"

"Hettie, it's good to see you as well. I thank you for your help." Brogan bowed his head in greeting. "Ella's fine, I think. She's trying to recover from using too much of her energy for the first time. I think it would be best if we got her inside."

"I agree. A little food and a good night's rest is what she needs most."

Ella watched Brogan and the witch talk. She followed most of their conversation, but her head was still spinning, and it was difficult to make sense of their words. She couldn't believe how exhausted she felt.

Brogan gave her a small nudge. "Come, little one. We'll go inside, and you can rest. Do you think you can walk?"

"I'll try, but you'll have to help me. Do you think it's normal to be so tired?" Ella attempted to stand, but when she got to her feet, she started to wobble. Brogan leaned in to help steady her, and Hettie stood on her other side.

It was Hettie who answered the question. "This is normal for your first time. The amulet will have made the connections in your body now, so the next time you'll recover much faster." The witch placed her hand under Ella's elbow to help keep her steady as they walked. "As I'm sure you've already guessed, I'm Hettie. It's good to meet you, Ella."

Ella could only nod. It took all her effort just to put one foot in front of the other. She still wasn't even sure what Hettie looked like, although she sounded very nice.

Ella noticed, as they walked, that they had entered another, smaller clearing. Directly in front of them was a small hill with a wooden hut leaning against it. As they approached the hut, Ella tried to get a better look at Hettie, but her eyes wouldn't focus. Silently they entered the hut. The walk had sapped Ella of any energy she'd regained.

Once inside, Ella realized why the hut was leaning on the hill—half the hill had become part of the living space. A large opening had been dug out of the side of the hill, with three smaller openings coming off the main one. A large, warm fire burned in the fireplace at the back; a small hole at the top of the hill allowed smoke to escape. In front of the fire were a wooden table and four chairs. Hettie led Ella to the table and pulled out a chair for her.

"I know you'd rather sleep right now than eat, but you really need to have something before you lie down. It'll help you regain your strength. I have a bed made up for you, so as soon as you're done eating, you can go lie down."

Hettie took a pot from its hook over the fire and ladled soup into a wooden bowl. She brought the bowl to Ella. "This is soup I made today. It's still quite warm, so be careful." Hettie handed a wooden spoon to Ella and sat in one of the other chairs while Ella ate.

Ella ate all the soup, but she wouldn't have been able to tell anyone what kind it was or how it tasted. She wasn't even sure if it smelled good or not. She was so exhausted that all her senses had shut down; she felt like her head was full of wool. She could barely keep her eyes open. If she didn't lie down soon, she'd drop where she was.

It vaguely registered that her body was once again moving. She was being led into the smallest of the smaller rooms. On the floor was a small bed, neatly made up.

"Brogan?"

"I'm here."

"Don't leave me, okay?"

"I won't. I'll be with you all night."

"Thank you." Her last words were only a whisper; she was already half-asleep. A soft brush of fur crossed her cheek before darkness completely closed in. It was sweet oblivion!

Chapter 28

Ella woke to the smell of something cooking. Still not completely awake, she was a little startled to find she wasn't in her own room at the tree hut. The memory of yesterday slowly crept in, and tears started to gather. Oh, how she hoped it was all just a bad dream! But judging by her surroundings, it'd all been real.

She looked around the small room and realized Brogan wasn't there. Before she could panic too much, she heard voices coming from the other room, one of which was Brogan's. Relief surged through her, and she took a few deep, calming breaths.

Ella got up and finger-combed her hair, trying to pull it off her face. Small pieces of grass, twigs, and dry leaves were tangled up in the back; without a brush, they'd be impossible to get out. She wished she'd remembered to bring a brush with her; why she hadn't, she would never know! She pulled a piece of ribbon from her pocket and tied her hair back as best she could. She then tried to smooth out the wrinkles in her long dress. It was no use. When you slept in your clothes, there was no hope of waking the next day looking fresh. *Well*, she thought, *here we go.*

She emerged into the main room and saw Brogan sitting in his preferred spot, next to the fire. Hettie was sitting at the table, holding a rather large cup. Brogan saw her first, and he stood up slowly to walk over to her.

"So you're awake at last. How did you sleep, Princess?"

"I slept soundly, thank you. I feel a little achy, though."

"Well, considering what we went through yesterday, if all you're feeling is a little achy, then you're doing rather well."

Hettie stood and smiled at Ella. "Perhaps we should talk about yesterday later, after you've had something to eat. You should go outside and refresh yourself first. There's a small building to the left, where you'll find all you need. When you're done, come back in, and I'll have something for you to eat."

Hettie gave Ella a motherly smile, took her hand, and escorted her to the door.

In the light of day, Ella got a good look at Hettie, who didn't look at all how Ella had envisioned. She looked much younger, and her eyes seemed to express great wisdom and warmth. They were the clearest color of light green Ella had ever seen. They also seemed very observant, as though they wouldn't miss much. Hettie was much taller than Ella had expected, and very slim. She was quite attractive for a witch. When Hettie grabbed her hand, Ella noticed that her touch was light and gentle yet firm. What surprised her most, though, was Hettie's hair. Why she'd thought Hettie would have long, dark hair, she didn't know. Hettie's hair was shoulder-length and light brown, with bright red highlights throughout. It wasn't all one length like Ella's but several different lengths all over. Hettie wore a plain black dress that covered her from her neck to her toes; it was so long that Ella wasn't even sure if Hettie wore anything on her feet.

Once they were outside, Hettie gestured in the direction Ella needed to go. Sure enough, on the left side of the front structure was a smaller hut leaning against the side of the hill. Ella had never seen a dwelling like this. It was most interesting.

She approached the smaller hut and pushed on the door. When it opened, she saw it was a small opening carved out of the hillside, just like in the bigger hut. There was only one small room, which had a tub that seemed to be made of wood, large enough to fit a person or a fairy. To the side of that was a ledge cut out from the hill that held a much smaller tub, also made of wood, with a small mirror hanging above it. On the other side of the room were two smaller carved-out openings that were both covered with dark curtains. When she opened the first one, she found a hand pump on the floor with a large bucket hanging over the spout; over the pump were three large shelves holding pieces of cut cloth for washing and drying and an assortment of handmade soaps. In the other curtained-off area was a wooden bench with a large hole cut into the top. Under the bench was another bucket. Ella was more than a little happy to see this bathroom after having had to go in the forest yesterday.

She used the small bathroom. Then, taking a little piece of cloth and some soap from the shelf, she pumped some water and cleaned herself as best she could. There was a short shelf just under the mirror, which she hadn't noticed when she first came in, that held a comb and brush. She brushed the forest debris from her hair and then tied it back up.

She'd just finished putting everything away when she heard a loud commotion outside. She stopped to listen more carefully and heard the loudest growl she'd heard yet come from Brogan. Fear coursed through her, and every nerve ending was on super-alert. The Silver Wings had found them!

Ella ran to the door and peeked out. There was no sense running headlong into danger or endangering Brogan further. At first she couldn't see anything but the forest that surrounded Hettie's home. When she stepped outside, she saw the back end of Brogan; he had someone or something backed into the corner of the hill and hut.

Hettie ran out of the main house, holding a strange, long pole in front of her like a shield. When she saw whom Brogan was holding hostage, she relaxed her grip on the pole.

"Mistress, tells this overgrown wolf that Is mean no harm. Tell hims that Is am with yous. Hes won't listen to mes. Hes believes Is am here to harm the princess fairy!"

"Brogan, it's safe. He's with me, and he's a friend! You can trust him. Please forgive me for not telling you I was expecting him." Hettie bowed her head to him apologetically. She bowed her head to Ella as well. "Please come inside, and I will make the introductions. Ella, you still need to eat." Hettie said this with a motherly smile. She then turned on her heel and walked back inside. She didn't even wait to see if Brogan was going to allow her friend to pass.

Brogan growled again and took several steps back. Now Ella could see who had caused the commotion. Still standing in the corner was the smallest man Ella had ever seen. He wasn't a fairy, that was for sure. His face looked middle-aged, but his body was no bigger than a child fairy. He had a long, dark beard with a long mustache going down either side of it. His hair was long and stringy and a shade lighter than his beard. His eyes were a glittering blue but revealed darker blue streaks when he turned his head. He wore a tunic of coarse brown material and a hat that covered only the back of his head. Ella wondered how the hat stayed on. That in itself was a marvel!

Brogan waited for Ella to join him. She could tell Brogan still didn't trust this little person and that he didn't want to leave her alone with him.

As soon as the strange little man saw Ella, he dropped to his knee and bowed before her. His head was still down when he started to speak, so Ella had to really listen to make out the words.

"Princess of the Blue Wings, it is a great honor to finally get to meet yous and to see yous up close. It will always be mys honor to serve yous if ever yous need mes!"

The little man stood up and indicated with his lowered head that she should go inside. Brogan let out another little growl and nosed Ella toward the door.

Chapter 29

Ella walked inside with Brogan on her heels, and the little man followed. Hettie had set the table and was pouring something into bowls. Whatever it was, it sure smelled good. Ella's tummy rumbled.

"Please, come in and sit. Vas, you arrived early; I didn't expect you until a little later. No matter; there's enough for us all. Ella, you can sit here. Now this isn't anything special, just some oats with dried fruits and nuts, but it'll fill you up!" Hettie pulled out a chair for Ella. Vas, the strange little man, sat opposite Ella.

"Brogan, I realize what I have to offer in the way of food isn't at all what a wolf would prefer. I'm sorry to say, I have nothing here at the moment that would be more to your taste! However, if you go to the first, larger clearing, where I met you yesterday, you'll find some plump deer grazing. When you arrive, two of the deer will remain when the others flee. I've used my magic to keep them there. One, of course, is for you, and the other is for us. That is, if you don't mind bringing one back for me? This way, I can make some stew for supper, and you'll have your meal as well."

Brogan looked at Hettie but said nothing. Ella knew he was unsure about leaving her alone, especially now that Vas had arrived. Hettie seemed to understand his reluctance.

"Brogan, my friend, if I'd wanted to hurt her, I would have done so already. Vas is a very close friend, and he'd rather see harm come to himself than to have anything happen to Ella." Hettie put her hand on Brogan's neck. "No harm will come to her in the short time you'll be away. I give you my word."

Brogan said nothing but bowed his head to acknowledge Hettie's words. Then he turned and walked out. Just on the other side of the door, he turned to look back. Hettie spoke again before he had time to say anything. "We won't speak of anything of importance until you return."

Brogan looked at Ella for a moment, and Ella winked. Brogan winked back and then ran off to find his meal.

While Brogan was away, no one said very much. Hettie, Ella, and Vas ate their breakfast and sat by the fire, sipping tea while they waited. Ella could tell Vas was a little uncomfortable with her there, although she wasn't sure why. She tried speaking to him a few times to put him at ease, but that seemed to make things worse. Whenever she spoke, he squirmed in his chair or gazed at the floor. She looked to Hettie for guidance, but Hettie's attention was elsewhere. She decided to stay silent until Brogan returned.

Less than an hour later, Brogan could be heard coming into the yard. He'd brought back the second deer for their evening meal.

Hettie went out to greet him and thanked him for bringing the deer. Ella and Vas followed her out. Ella watched as Hettie retrieved a rope made of tree roots and tied one end to the deer's back legs, hanging it from a nearby tree. Hettie efficiently handled the deer to prepare it for their meal later on.

"Well, my friends, this should hang for a few hours before we cut it up. Vas, would you please take this hide and string it for me? I want to make Ella a protective cloak with it." Hettie smiled at Ella. "While Vas is doing this, we can start our little talk. Vas will join us when he's done. It won't take him long." Hettie put her arm around Ella's shoulders, steering them both back to the hut. Hettie looked back to see if Brogan was following, though she needn't have bothered. Brogan was only two steps behind Ella.

Chapter 30

Once inside, Hettie took a thick blanket from the foot of her own bed. Beside the bed was a covered basket, which she also picked up. "Perhaps we should go out and sit on the top of the hill for our little talk. It's such a nice day, and there's no reason why we shouldn't enjoy it."

Brogan and Ella followed Hettie up a small path leading to the hilltop. Several small trees were there, as well as an open area where Hettie laid out the blanket, overlooking part of the forest. The view was spectacular. Ella sat on the blanket; Hettie sat across from her, and Brogan laid down beside Ella.

"I have quite a lot to tell you, so I'm going to get straight to the point! Ella, you are young, but already you have so many responsibilities, with more to come very soon. The danger you're in is so enormous it makes it that much more difficult to protect you. What happened yesterday was only the beginning. You were blessed to get Brogan as your guardian; without him, you wouldn't have survived your encounter yesterday."

"You know what the worst part about yesterday is?" Ella looked at both Brogan and Hettie. "I recognized a couple of the Silver Wings who attacked us. One used to live in our village and isn't that much older than me."

"They fear you, and, since the stories of the Blue Wings are still being told, they see you as the enemy." Hettie smiled sadly at Ella. "They don't all feel this way, but many still do."

Hettie looked out over the forest for a moment. "I know it's difficult, but we can't dwell on what happened yesterday. We must focus on you. You must learn all you are capable of and how all the gifts you have been given work. This is something I can help you with. Also, you must learn the history of your ancestors and how what happened then affects you now."

"I already know a little of what happened to the Blue Wings and the prophecy that was written. I'm the child whom the Blue Wings elder spoke of, and I'm the one to continue the bloodline of the Blue Wings." Ella put her hand next to Brogan's front leg. His presence gave her comfort.

"You were told of the legend, and you were told of how the Silver Wings wiped out the Blue Wings for no other reason but fear. Fear of what they didn't understand. It was the hope of the Blue Wings that, if given time, the Silver Wings would grow and become more understanding. For some Silver Wings, that happened; but for others, time has changed nothing. So many were affected by the Silver Wings' actions back then, and those effects are still felt today!" Hettie closed her eyes for a moment. Ella could see she was trying to hold back tears. She reached out to comfort Hettie, but Hettie began to speak again with her eyes still closed.

"I know that Brogan told you about my sister. She was a good person, and she loved everything and everyone. I see a lot of her in you, Ella." Hettie opened her eyes. "She had a good heart and cared for all living creatures; she trusted all those around her. Like my sister, you need to realize not all creatures are worthy of your trust, and not all creatures have only good intentions. There will always be those who look you in the eye and call you friend but secretly wish you great harm. My sister couldn't forgive herself and felt she was completely to blame for the demise of the Blue Wings.

She hadn't met them, but she knew I was very close to them and spent much of my time in their company."

Ella was in complete shock, and that was putting it mildly. She thought she had prepared herself for what Hettie had to say, but this wasn't at all what she'd expected.

"I know this must be somewhat of a surprise for you. My friendship with the Blue Wings was not well known. Eamon was a very close friend. And, being a close friend, he was concerned that our friendship might endanger me. His concern for my safety was why so few knew of our friendship." Hettie looked up to the sky.

"My sister wasn't aware there was so much hate toward the Blue Wings. She really had no understanding of hate; she loved all living things. When she was approached by a Silver Wing, he asked her to lend him some powerful magic that would help destroy a dangerous foe. She asked about the enemy and was told that, for her own safety, it would be best if she knew very little. This Silver Wing was well known to her, as they'd had dealings with each other in the past, so she had no reason to question his honesty or his intentions. She gladly helped him. She also knew the Silver Wings had gotten help from others; the elves, gnomes, and goblins had given some of their magic to help the Silver Wings as well. She believed she was helping a friend in need. It wasn't until the Blue Wings were wiped out that my sister discovered what her magic had truly been used for. It was too late for her to do anything to change the outcome. Since she knew of my friendship with the Blue Wings, the guilt became too much. She couldn't live with what she'd done. I didn't find out about my sister until after the fact, and by then it was too late for me to do anything. Vas came shortly after my sister's death to explain what she'd done. He also told me of his involvement." Hettie stopped abruptly. "It's a story you must hear from him."

Hettie waved her hand to Vas, indicating that he should come over. He'd been standing behind them, listening. Ella watched him walk toward them; he looked like he was walking to his death. He dragged his feet and walked as slowly as he could without actually stopping. It was obvious he didn't want to be there and that whatever his story was, he certainly didn't want to tell it.

"Vas, don't worry; I'll be here with you." Hettie gently guided Vas to the blanket and pulled him down beside her. Vas looked up at Hettie, who gave him a reassuring smile, then looked back down at the blanket. He played with the edge of the blanket and pulled at the grass.

"Is am an elf. There was a time Is was a chief of mys people. The Silver Wings had come and ask mes for help. Theys say theys need help to defeat theirs enemy. I'ms the chief and understand the need to destroy the enemy, so Is give thems the magic theys need. Is believe Is am helping." Vas's voice cracked. He cleared his throat before continuing.

"Is knew the Blue Wings well; in fact, theys helped our people many times. Made us better when wes was sick and helped us to find food when things were not good. The Blue Wings elder was a good man. When Is help the Silver Wings, mys people shun mes and put a curse on mes. Now, I'ms to walk with my shame of what Is done, until Is make it right. Is didn't know Is was helping Silver Wings hurt Blue Wings. If Is had known, Is would never have given thems elfin magic."

Vas turned away from Ella. "Is wandered the forest for several days when Is met Mari. Is stayed with hers for many weeks before hers guilt overcame hers. Shes sent mes on an errand the day shes ended hers life. Shes knew Is would stop hers. Is was the one to find hers. Is searched for days looking for Mari's sister. When Is found hers, Is told hers of ours sad deeds. Is vowed to help until Is make things right. Is have been with mys mistress for many years."

For the first time, Vas looked Ella in the eye. "Princess, Is will help to protect yous until mys days are over. I'ms so sorry for what Is have help to do to yous and yours. Is promise to help yous in any way Is can." Vas lowered his eyes and said no more.

There was a moment of silence before Ella felt compelled to speak. "What happened all those years ago was terrible, and the blame for it lies solely with those few Silver Wings. They are the ones who should feel this guilt and be held accountable for their actions. They would have done anything to gain the power they needed, and they did. They lied and tricked those who they called friends and perhaps would have harmed those who went against them. What happened back then cannot be undone. All we can do is learn from that time and try to ensure it won't happen again. Vas, I hold no ill will toward you and forgive you for your mistake. You need to forgive yourself. It is time now for us all to move forward."

Vas looked at Ella for a moment and then stood up and quietly walked away. His shoulders were shaking, and Ella could tell he was crying. She wanted to comfort him, but she knew he needed time to compose himself and work out his grief on his own. He would be embarrassed and feel even greater shame for his tears if she approached.

She turned her attention to Hettie. "If you were close to the Blue Wings, you must know a great deal about them!"

"Yes, I do. But first I must talk to you about your gifts."

Chapter 31

"You've been born with all the Blue Wings' abilities. However, I'm guessing you haven't had time to become aware of all the abilities you possess. So let's start off with the ones you do know about. Tell me the ones you are already aware of."

"Well, let me think. The first ability that came to me was my ability to become invisible. I can speak to all animals, even the smallest creatures. I'm able to move small objects with my thoughts. I can sense when others are coming, even when they're a great distance away." Ella paused for a moment. "Well, I thought that was one of my abilities, but now that I think about it, I didn't know Vas was coming. I hadn't sensed him at all, and I didn't sense the Silver Wings in the forest."

"You didn't sense Vas because I cloaked his energy field, and, I don't know how, but the Silver Wings were cloaked too. Normally you are able to sense others' energy fields, and all creatures have a distinct energy force they give off. All energies you come in contact with you'll remember. If you recall, you had no idea I was in the clearing with you last night. I have the ability to cloak our energy so no others can sense us or know we are near."

Hettie glanced in the direction Vas had gone. "You should know I've had Vas following and watching over you. He has been from the day Brogan came into your life. Brogan can protect you from physical danger, but he cannot know what others say or do when you're not around. This is why Vas has been watching and listening to all those around you. You need to be aware that there are a few in your village who, even now, are trying to find a way to destroy you. At this time, we're unsure who those fairies are, but they do exist. Brogan is the main reason you haven't been harmed."

Ella couldn't hide her shock and dismay. She already knew in her heart this was true, but it was still difficult to hear. Some of her own people had turned against her! She felt like she'd been punched in the stomach, and her heart felt like it might burst.

"I'm so sorry, Ella. It's better to know the truth now so you can be prepared." Hettie squeezed Ella's hand.

Brogan spoke for the first time. "You should have told me Vas was watching over Ella; it would've been better for all of us. There were times when I felt him, but I couldn't see anyone. I knew we were being watched! Do you realize how much extra strain you placed on us?" His tone clearly conveyed his anger.

"We couldn't tell you, Brogan. It was safer for everyone this way. I'm sorry, my friend, but it was my decision to keep Vas's presence unknown."

Brogan snarled, unhappy with this news.

"Ella, I know this is a difficult time, but I need us to continue. What other abilities do you know about?"

It took Ella a moment before she could bring herself to speak. Brogan nudged her hand with his nose for support.

"I know I can heal. I'm not sure to what extent, but for small injuries, I'm able to help. I know things without any reason for the knowledge." Ella thought for a second. "I can hear the thoughts of others, but so far this has happened with only a few fairies. Also, I can create a force of energy to knock out those who want to hurt me. It's like a shockwave of energy, I guess. Those are all I know of."

"You've learned quite a few already, more than I expected in such a short time. This is good. Normally you would learn of the others when it was time, but time is something we don't have right now. So I'll tell you of your other abilities, because you'll need to work on them to become stronger and more comfortable using them. Also, with time and practice, your abilities will grow and increase in strength. Are you ready to hear them now?"

"I guess so."

"You'll be able to communicate with all living things, including grass, trees, and insects. If it's living, you'll be able to speak to it." Hettie paused to think and then continued. "As you already know, you can throw out an energy blast, but with that same energy, you'll be able to create a protective shield around a small area. The size of the shield will grow as you grow in strength. Also, when it's time, you'll be able to mentally call to other Blue Wings—and there are others out there. You'll be able to communicate with others over long distances with your mind, but you must have a clear picture of whom you wish to communicate with. They will hear you and be able to speak back to you without saying a word. You also have the power to stop time for short periods. This ability is one you won't want to use very often. When you stop time or alter time in any way, there could be serious effects that you weren't aware of or that you even considered. You must always use this ability with caution."

"I can stop time?" Ella was shocked.

"Yes, and you can travel with thought. If you picture where it is you want to be, you'll go there. This is another ability you must use with caution, because you'll never know what awaits you when you arrive at your thought destination. You could appear into a dangerous situation. Also, you must always be very clear in your mind where it is you want to be, or you could end up in the wrong place."

Hettie waited to see if Ella had anything to say. She looked a little shell-shocked, and Hettie was sure that if she did have any questions, they wouldn't come until later. She needed time to digest everything.

"Ella, you have much to think over, so I'll leave you here with Brogan for a while. In this basket you'll find some dried fruit and fresh cheese. There's also some bread I made yesterday. If you're hungry, please help yourself. I need to go start our supper."

Hettie got up and put her hand on Ella's shoulder. "There's still so much I have to tell you, but I believe you need time before you hear anymore. Perhaps if you're feeling up to it, you can practice some of your new abilities."

Hettie squeezed Ella's shoulder before she turned to Brogan. "I had my reasons for keeping silent about Vas. I hope you can forgive me."

Hettie walked back down the path, Vas following close behind.

"Did you know about all my abilities?" Ella looked carefully at Brogan.

"I was told of some, but not all. I didn't know you could travel with thought or that you could stop time."

Brogan gave Ella that lopsided grin she didn't like. "That one sure would've come in handy yesterday." Brogan let out a little half-laugh/half-growl to lighten the mood. Ella shook her head and playfully punched him in the shoulder.

Chapter 32

Ella and Brogan continued talking as the day went on. "Well, this has been an informative and interesting day so far." Ella looked out over the forest, pulling on the grass at the edge of the blanket. "I knew there were some in my clan who disliked me, but I wouldn't have believed any of them would really hurt me. I wonder who they might be."

"I don't know, but whoever threw that rock meant to hit you. I think that's a clear indication you're no longer safe there—we didn't need Hettie to tell us that. Fear is a powerful thing and can make even the best of us react in the worst of ways." Brogan put his paw over Ella's hand for a moment.

"I just feel sick! My own people! My own clan! What about my parents? Will these same fairies hurt them to get to me? Brogan, we need to go back and get them, and we need to find another place to go."

"What we need to do is hear the rest of what Hettie has to say. Then we can make plans. I believe your parents are safe for the time being. The ones who want to hurt you are looking for you right now; they aren't focused on your parents. We'll ensure their safety when the time comes. We can't make any rash decisions; that will only put you in more danger." Brogan pressed Ella's hand with his paw. "Your parents are safe right now. We must think of what's best for you, and going back to that village isn't safe."

Ella said nothing. She knew Brogan was right, but it didn't mean she wasn't going to worry.

Ella and Brogan stayed on the hill for almost an hour. Ella didn't eat anything; she was far too upset. She didn't try to use any of her abilities, either; she just wasn't able to focus. All she could think about was what happened yesterday and her parents' safety.

When they came down from the hill, they went inside. Hettie was busy preparing the evening meal. Ella offered to help, but Hettie said she was almost done. Feeling a little lost, Ella wandered back outside and sat in the small clearing in front of the hut. Her whole life had changed in just a few days, and she wasn't happy about these changes. Normally she was a very positive fairy, but with all that had happened, staying positive was difficult to do! The attack yesterday was the most difficult to understand. If they'd gotten her, she wouldn't have seen another day. Why? Because her wings had turned blue! It all seemed like a bad dream.

Ella was so deep in thought that when she felt a hand on her shoulder, she jumped. Looking up, she saw Hettie. "I'm so sorry to startle you; I thought you heard me come out. May I sit with you for a while?"

"Of course. I was just thinking about everything that's happened."

"I know how difficult everything's been. Yesterday must have been a real shock, and my news today is not much better. I believe it's far better to be aware and be prepared. I'm sorry I've caused you further pain. If this is any help, I think most of your clan, although they're having a difficult time with your differences, are very much against seeing harm done to you." Hettie gave Ella a small smile. "You still have a lot to learn in a very short time, and, if you're worrying about your parents' safety, you won't be able to focus on anything but them. That's why I took it upon myself to cast a protection spell over them, which will keep them safe until you reunite. I also did a protection spell for your keeper of the fire, as I understand that because of your relationship, she may also be in danger."

"Oh, Hettie, thank you so much! You have no idea how much this means to me." Ella was almost in tears.

"You don't have to thank me. I was glad to do it. You should know that I also cast one for Brogan, although I'm not sure he really needs one. He's very good at protecting himself." Hettie winked at Ella. "I also tried casting one for you—several times, in fact—but no matter what I did, the spell wouldn't work. I've never had this happen before. You'll have to be extra careful, although with your own powers and Brogan watching over you, I think you might be safer than anyone else."

"Why wouldn't the spell work for me?"

"I'm not sure. I've done this spell many times and never had this happen before."

"It's okay. I have my protection in the form of a giant wolf!"

They both looked at Brogan, who was lying in the shade not far from them. It was one of those times when he looked like he was sleeping, but Ella could sense he was wide awake and very aware.

"Hettie, can I ask you something?"

"Of course. You can ask me anything."

"Do I have a choice in any of this?"

"What do you mean?" Hettie looked surprised.

"I mean, do I have a choice? What if I don't want this 'gift' I've been given? What if I don't want to be the Blue Wing Princess or to have the responsibilities? Maybe I don't want all the Blue Wings' abilities. Because I don't! I don't want my blue wings, and I don't want to be hunted down like some kind of animal. Is that wrong? Am I a bad fairy because I don't?" Ella felt hysterical. Tears poured down her face.

Hettie looked stunned. "Ella, I'm not sure what to say."

"I feel like everything is out of control, and there's nothing I can do to get that control back. Those fairies in the woods were trying to kill me! If they had their way, I wouldn't be here right now." Ella covered her face with her hands and cried.

Brogan sat up, watching them. Hettie motioned him to stay back.

"Ella, I want you to know that what happened in the woods was a terrible thing. You wouldn't be normal if it didn't have an effect on you."

Hettie put her arm around Ella and gave her a squeeze. "Frankly, it's not wrong for you to feel the way you do, and it doesn't make you a bad fairy. The thing is, none of us have a choice right now. This is the way it is. You are the Blue Wing Princess, and you have all the responsibilities that go with that position. You don't have to like it, but it is what it is. What's happening scares us all, Ella, but we must keep going forward. Things will get better; you'll see."

They sat there for a little while, Ella crying and Hettie holding her until the tears ended. When Ella had a hold of herself once more, she looked up at Hettie.

"I'm sorry, Hettie. I just feel a little overwhelmed. Please don't think any less of me."

"There's nothing you can do to make me think less of you! How you feel is normal, and I would wonder if you didn't feel this way." Hettie gave Ella another squeeze.

"Thank you for listening." Ella felt a little better.

"There's one more thing. I think it's a good idea to contact your parents and let them know you're safe. I'm sure they worry as much about you as you do about them. You'll be here for a few days before we decide what to do next, and there's still much I need to talk to you about. After all you've been through, I think talking with them will help make you feel a little better, too!"

"Maybe you're right. I've never been away from them before, and I miss them terribly. It would help if I could talk to them." Ella paused. "I'm not really sure I understand how this ability works. Are you sure I can do this if I've had no inclination of having such a power?"

Hettie smiled. "I'm very sure you're capable. You just need to clear your mind of all else and concentrate on the image of your mother. You'll both know when you make the connection; you'll feel it. It is through you and your connection that she will be able to communicate. You don't need to speak out loud; you can speak with your minds. In fact, it'd be a good idea to tell her not to speak out loud. If anyone were to see or hear her, it may create even more problems. It could potentially put her in danger."

Hettie stood up and brushed the grass from her long skirt. She was just about to leave, but at the last second, she turned to look at Ella again.

"Ella, every one of the abilities I told you about, you possess. You must believe in yourself and in what you're capable of. Look deep inside yourself, and you'll know it's true. Always remember that we believe in you." Hettie walked back to the hut.

Chapter 33

Ella sat down beside Brogan. They sat in comfortable silence for a while. Even though they hadn't been together long, Ella felt comfort and strength being with him.

"Are you all right, little one?"

"I think so. I was just having a moment."

"There's nothing wrong with having a moment."

"I want to try to talk to my mother, to reassure her and let her know we'll be here several more days. I won't tell her about what happened yesterday, though. That would only worry her. I'll tell her more when we know more. The thing is, she's not going to be happy no matter what I say."

"I think speaking with her would be good." Brogan slid closer to Ella and brushed her shoulder with his head. "I'm sorry it must be this way, but everything will work out in the end; you'll see."

Ella silently nodded. "Before I forget, I want to thank you for all you did yesterday. If it wasn't for you, I wouldn't be here."

"Please don't thank me. I'd rather die than see something happen to you."

Ella wasn't sure, but she thought she saw tears in Brogan's eyes; but he turned his head away too quickly for her to be sure. A moment later, he turned his head back to her. "Besides, perhaps there'll come a day when you'll have to save me." He wiggled his eyebrows and smiled.

Ella giggled. "I'm sure that would never happen! You can take care of yourself quite well."

"You never know."

"Well, I guess I should try to reach my parents."

Ella took several breaths and closed her eyes. Getting a mental picture of her mother, she let her thoughts drift out, but nothing happened. Feeling frustrated, she took several more deep breaths, this time letting each breath out very slowly. Again she got a clear picture of her mother and reached out to her with her thoughts. This time, she could physically feel her mind traveling through the forest and into their little village. It was a very strange feeling when the distinct mental connection was made and her mother's thoughts connected with her own. Using her mind as her mouth, she began to speak.

"Mother, can you hear me?"

"Ella, oh, thank goodness! Are you all right? Where are you?"

Ella could see everything so clearly in her mind; it was like she was really there. She could see her mother in their tree hut kitchen, and her father was coming in. Her father was saying something, but because she wasn't connected with him, she was unable to hear his words. Her mother replied to his question. "It's Ella, but I don't know where she is."

"Mother, listen to me. I'm talking to you through thought. It seems I have many abilities, and this is one of them. Brogan and I are still with Hettie, and we need to be here for several more days."

"You're still with the witch? Then how can you be speaking with me?"

"It's one of my abilities. I'm connected to you with my thoughts."

"That's an interesting ability. Wait, what do you mean, several more days? Why in fairydom must you stay for that long? This wasn't mentioned in that message she sent, so what's going on?"

"Listen, everything is fine! Hettie's very nice, and I quite like her; she's been very helpful. Before you say anything else, can you please do me a favor? When you speak to me, can you try not to say the words out loud? If someone overhears you, it could put you in danger. Just think what you want to say, and I'll hear you. We're connected through our minds."

"Well, if I don't say the words out loud, how will your father know what's going on? Plus, we're at home; who'll hear us here? I'm not sure how someone hearing me talk to you would put me in danger. That's a little crazy, don't you think?"

"Mother, please, this is important. I'll explain everything to you later, but for right now, just think your thoughts, and you can tell Father after."

Ella heard her mother explaining to her father what she'd just said. She waited until her mother was finished before she spoke to her again.

"I need to stay here a few more days. It's very important, and the information Hettie is giving me has already helped me tremendously. Please don't try to look for me; it wouldn't be wise and could possibly put us all in danger. It's only for a few more days, and I'll connect with you again before we leave. I want you to know I'm perfectly safe. Nothing will happen to me while I'm here."

"I don't like this, Ella. What's so important that you must stay longer? What information is the witch giving you?"

"The witch has a name. Her name is Hettie, and she happens to be very caring. Mother, please, I'll explain everything to you when I get back, I promise. It would take too long to tell you now."

She could tell her mother wanted to argue the point. It would be better for both of them if she kept this conversation short.

"Ella, I think . . ."

"Mother, please, let it go! I'm well, and all is fine. I'll contact you in a few days. You don't need to worry about me; everything's fine."

"I don't like you being so far away!"

"I miss you, too, more than you know. I have to go. I love you. Tell Father I send my love."

"You be careful, young fairy, do you hear me? I love you, too, sweetheart, and we'll talk in a few days."

Ella opened her eyes and felt the connection between them end. She slumped forward and sighed. That had been the strangest feeling she'd ever experienced—like she was a part of her mother's mind, a part of her thoughts. She wondered if the feeling had been the same for her mother. Just the thought of that gave her a shiver. This ability was one she wouldn't want to use very often, at least not with her mother.

Brogan was watching Ella closely and knew the moment their connection ended. "Your mother took the news well?"

"As well as she ever does." She gave a half-hearted little laugh. "Brogan, can I ask you something?"

"Of course. You can ask me anything, although there's no guarantee I'll have the answer."

"I've only been away from my parents for a few days, and I miss them. Don't you miss your family and friends?"

Brogan was not at all prepared for this question. It took him a moment to collect his thoughts. "I have no family, nor do I have what you would consider friends."

"What do you mean, you have no family? So you just magically appeared one day?"

"I was taken at a young age from my mother so I could be trained in the ways of a warrior. That was, and is, my destiny. We don't have friendships or attachments. I have my warrior brothers, but we've been trained not to get emotionally involved. The purpose of this is so when and if something were to happen to one of us, we would not be hindered by our grief. Our first priority is always our assignments. I would be unable to do my job properly if I were consumed with such emotions. It's the way we are, and it's what we are trained to do."

"That sounds so cold. You're trained not to have feelings? How can that be? It's not natural not to have feelings. Haven't you ever thought about having a family of your own one day?"

"I've no need for a family. A family would only tie me down and hinder me. I'd no longer be able to do what I was trained to do. Only a select few warrior wolves are chosen to mate with a female. It's how our clan ensures our bloodline remains pure and strong. Then only the biggest and strongest pups are taken from the litter and trained. It's our way."

"It still sounds cold to me. So I'm your assignment, your job?"

"Yes, but with you, it's much different, because we've connected. This connection is rare, and I don't know much about it." Brogan cleared his throat. "Does this answer your question?"

"I guess, except the part about our connection. How does this make it different?"

"Perhaps we could talk about this another time."

Brogan was clearly uncomfortable with this conversation. It was no wonder, considering his past.

"I must feel this connection the same way you do, right?" Ella waited for him to respond, but he only nodded. "Even though we've only been together for a short time, I can't imagine my life without you. As far as I'm concerned, you do have a family. You have me! I'd also like to point out that my feelings for you, my parents, or anyone else aren't a hindrance to me. They don't hinder me or lessen my ability to do what I must!"

Ella smiled. "I'm not sure what I'd do without you now, so you better always be safe. I just thought I should tell you that." She gave him a big hug.

Brogan stiffened and sat rock-still until the hug was over. Ella could have sworn she saw tears in his eyes again. The warrior wolf brought to tears by an itty-bitty fairy! For the first time since leaving her parents, Ella felt a little better.

If only she could have seen into the future.

Chapter 34

The stew Hettie made was delicious, and Ella had a second helping. By the time they were finished, Ella wasn't sure if she was going to be able to get up from the table—that was how much she'd eaten. Everyone pitched in to clean up except for Brogan, who had gone outside to eat his own meal.

When Brogan was finished, he came back in and found everyone sitting at the table, waiting for him. Hettie had decided to tell Ella a little more that night.

"There's so much more I need to share with you, and I don't want to leave it too long or we may run out of time. It wouldn't do to have you go without all this information. I want to tell you about Eamon, your ancestor and my good friend." Hettie walked over to the fire. She fed it some small pieces of wood. "Eamon's care and concern for others was one of a kind! When we first met, I felt like we'd known each other all our lives. He accepted me for who I was and didn't judge me because I was a witch, like many others did. He always made time for others and would listen if you just wanted to talk. He was an exceptional person. After all these years, I still miss him dearly."

Hettie turned and looked directly at Ella. "I'm telling you this not because it is relevant to what I need to say, but because it's important that you understand how I fit in back then." Hettie turned back to the fire. She seemed to find it easier to speak when she looked into the flames.

"The amulet you wear is infused with all of the Blue Wings' power and knowledge, which have been carried down from generation to generation. Eamon told me he was creating the amulet for the future so he could ensure that his knowledge, and the knowledge of all Blue Wings, would never be totally lost. I hadn't known then that he understood his time with us was ending, but he did know, and he prepared carefully for it. Perhaps he never told me because he knew what I would do. I would have tried to stop it. He made sure the day the Silver Wings came for him that I was very far away. I suspected something was wrong, but when I would ask, Eamon would tell me all was well and not to worry!"

Hettie looked at Brogan. "He asked me to go with him when he went to speak with the leader of the warrior-wolf tribe, and I was there when he spoke to Ulrike. That is your leader's name, yes?"

Brogan nodded. "He's been the leader of the warrior wolves for many, many years."

"Perhaps he's as old as me." Hettie looked back at the fire. "Eamon explained to Ulrike that the Silver Wings were allowing their fears to control their actions and that it would be only a matter of time before something happened. Ulrike offered to protect Eamon and the Blue Wings, but Eamon declined his help and asked only if he'd be willing to ensure that the wolf pack helped at a future time. Ulrike agreed to be there for Eamon in the future."

Hettie stopped talking for a moment. At some point she'd closed her eyes, and the memories of that time played across the back of her eyelids. She hadn't been prepared for how difficult it was to speak about this out loud. Vulnerability wasn't something she allowed herself to feel, and she tried never to show it in the presence of others. This show of emotion wouldn't do any of them any good. She gave herself a mental shake.

"When I questioned Eamon about his visit with Ulrike, he said only, 'I'm ensuring the future of my kind and preparing for a future that is so far ahead I couldn't possibly be here to see it. Sometimes, losing a fight doesn't mean you've lost the battle. So it's always important to pick your battles carefully, to ensure victory when your opponent least expects it. Preparation is the key, Hettie, never forget that!' He said nothing more, and I never knew what he was talking about until it was too late." Hettie returned to the table and sat down.

"The second time he asked me to go with him to the clan of the warrior wolves, he wouldn't allow me to go in with him when he spoke to Ulrike. He'd brought with him a journal of some kind, which he took in with him; he didn't have it when he came out. Just as we were about to leave, he called Ulrike and handed him the amulet you now wear." Hettie pointed to the amulet around Ella's neck.

"He told Ulrike that all the answers for his future princess could be found with that amulet. It was planned, his handing that amulet to Ulrike with me to witness it. When we returned to his village, he told me that he and I would be entwined in this life and in all our lives to follow. True friendship does not end; it lasts forever. He then explained all of his abilities and what the amulet represented. I asked him why he would share such things with me, and he said it's what true friends do. They share."

Hettie covered her face with her hands. Tears started to gather. It'd been so long since she'd cried that she'd believed it was something she wasn't capable of anymore. Apparently, she was wrong. The first tear slid down her cheek. She tried to wipe it away before anyone noticed, but she wasn't fast enough—Ella saw it.

By that one tear, Ella knew Hettie's presence in her life was important and that her motivation to help was truly sincere. Until that moment, Ella hadn't completely trusted Hettie; but now she knew she'd never again question her trust. Hettie smiled at her. A true bond between them had formed.

"Witches have always been known to have long lives. However, the amount of time I've walked this earth is exceptionally long, even for a witch. I knew the moment of Eamon's demise, because at the moment of his death I felt the gift he'd left to me. It was the gift of energy, strength, and power. He's the reason for my exceptionally long life. He wanted to ensure I was still here to help Ella.

"The night of his death, he came to me in a dream. He explained that he'd given me the gift of life so that I might be able to give his future daughter the gift of life as well. He told me that now wasn't the time for him to fight this battle. It wasn't his destiny. There would come a time for this battle to be fought, and it would be his future daughter's destiny to fight it. She would need help, though, and he'd done all he could to ensure the help she needed would be here.

"I, of course, wanted to destroy all those who had destroyed the Blue Wings. He told me not to let revenge rule my heart and mind. It would do no good. Fear was powerful and could make even the best of us do terrible things and react in terrible ways. He was right. Throughout my life, I've seen what fear can do. I've seen fear rule and ruin the lives of many. It's now time to fight that fear and show those who allow it to rule their lives that there are other options." Hettie was looking only at Ella when she said this, and she took Ella's hand.

"I see fear in your eyes, Ella. Fear for your destiny, fear of the unknown, and fear for those you love. It's normal to feel fear, but don't ever let it overtake you or rule your actions. Don't make decisions based on fear, and don't second-guess yourself because of it. You're not alone; you never have been."

Hettie released Ella's hand. "Your connection to your ancestors is in your amulet. Believe and trust in it. Once you do that, you might find that some of the answers will follow."

Hettie stood and stretched. She walked around the table to hug Ella. "I do believe that's enough for tonight. We'll talk more tomorrow. If ever you feel you need to talk, I'm always willing to listen." Hettie kissed Ella's forehead. "Sleep well, little one."

PART 3

DECEPTION

Chapter 35

Not long after their talk, Hettie went to bed, and Ella decided to do the same. As she lay in the dark, she held onto the amulet and thought about everything Hettie had told her. There was so much to think about that she didn't think she'd sleep at all. To help clear her mind, she concentrated on the sounds around her. Brogan was staying with her again, and she could hear his breathing even out with sleep. Slowly, his even breaths lulled her to sleep. Her last thought before drifting off was of the amulet and its powers, perhaps because she still held the amulet tightly in her hand.

She knew she was dreaming. Nothing around her was really different, not in the way dreams tended to change things, but she still knew it was a dream. She was sitting by the fire in Hettie's kitchen. She felt warm and cozy, listening to the fire crackle and pop as the sap in the logs caught on fire. Everything else around her was quiet. It took a few moments, but she finally realized Brogan wasn't with her, which was strange; he was never far from her side. A thread of fear started to take hold, but, with a small mental shake, she reminded herself she was still at Hettie's and that nothing would happen while she was there. In fact, she was safer there than anywhere else.

Having eased her fears, she settled down before the fire, allowing the dancing flames to mesmerize her. It took her a while to realize she was no longer alone; someone was now sitting at the table with her. She couldn't see who it was, because his face was in shadow. Strangely enough, his presence caused her no distress. Any fear she had all but vanished, and a feeling of calmness, light, love, and warmth filled her, making her smile. Even though she couldn't see his face, she felt sure she knew who was sitting with her.

Eamon got up from his chair and kneeled before her. He took her hands in his. Tears ran freely down his face.

It was so strange to actually see him; he was nothing like she'd imagined him. He was a little round and rather short. He had the same light golden-brown hair she did and the same dark-blue eyes. She'd pictured him blond with brown eyes, and definitely taller. His face was round like the rest of him, with small lines carved around his eyes and mouth. Laugh lines, her mother would call them. His eyes shone with kindness and love.

He leaned forward and kissed her on the cheek. "I have waited a very long time for you, my daughter." His voice was deep and melodious.

With that kiss, Ella felt strength enter and flow through her. The feeling, though good, was a little overwhelming, and her own eyes started to tear up.

"I know what I ask of you is great. I've placed upon you a great responsibility. However, I have not given you anything you cannot handle, and I know nothing that comes your way will be too much for you to deal with. You have within the best of us all, and I believe there's nothing you can't do." He squeezed her hands.

"It wasn't time to confront the Silver Wings' fear when I walked among them. We all needed time, knowledge, and growth. The path you walk will not always be easy, but you'll never walk alone. I have always been with you, and I always will be. The amulet, which I made just for you, will allow you to contact me anytime."

Eamon pointed at the amulet around Ella's neck. "That amulet is very powerful and contains all the Blue Wings' knowledge and strength. The amulet carries with it the essence of all Blue Wings and will help guide you on your path." Eamon walked to the fire and gazed into it for just a moment before he turned to look at Ella again.

"Your warrior wolf would give his life for you. Not because it's his duty, but because you are the only one he has ever let into his heart. Hettie would do all in her power to protect you. Not because I asked it of her, but because you have given her trust and hope. She, too, holds you close to her heart. Your parents, Story Teller, and even Vas are all willing to stand beside you and fight for what's right. These are all the hearts you have touched without even trying. Think of all you might accomplish if you try." He returned to the table and took Ella's hand again.

"Your life is about to change immensely, much sooner than even I had thought. It saddens me that you are unable to return to your village, but doing so would jeopardize your safety. Those few against you have had time to spread their fears to others, and the safety of the innocent would also be at risk. It's time for you to go to your true home, Ella, where you belong, and where you can start the healing process."

Eamon pointed to the fire. Above the flames, which had turned the color of every blue imaginable, was an image of the Blue Wings' village. Ella couldn't see it clearly, but she knew she knew it better than the village she had grown up—it was home!

"What about my parents and Story Teller? I must go back to get them. They're also in great danger."

Eamon explained what would happen. "You'll hold Brogan around the neck. Be sure both arms are around him and both your hands can touch. With your thoughts, you will travel to the Blue Wings' village. Brogan must travel with you for your continued safety.

"Hettie will get your parents. Story Teller, too, if she chooses to leave, but that choice will be hers to make. They'll meet you two days after you reach the village. You'll leave the day after tomorrow. Remember, unseen eyes are continually watching and gathering information about your plans to take back to the others. Those eyes will not be able to see you once you get to the Blue Wings' village.

"Before you leave, you must contact your mother as you did yesterday and explain what is to happen. Ask her to speak with Story Teller. If your keeper of the fire wishes to come, she should be with your parents when Hettie and Vas arrive. Don't try to contact any others from your parents' village, as we don't know whom we can trust. Hettie has already agreed to do what is needed. She'll be staying with you at our village to guide you. You must not fear for those you love; everything will be taken care of."

Eamon pulled Ella up. He looked at her for a silent moment. "The love I feel for you, my daughter, cannot be expressed. If ever there's a time you feel overwhelmed or fearful, just hold onto the amulet, and you'll feel the warmth of my love and the strength it brings. No matter the outcome, I'll always love you and be proud of you. The goodness you have within will spill out and show all creatures big or small there is hope for the future."

Eamon took Ella into a fatherly embrace and held her for a moment before reluctantly letting go. "Sleep well, my daughter, and may your dreams be only happy ones."

Before Ella could respond, he was gone. The room was empty once again, and the fire in the hearth had returned to its original color. Ella sat back down at the table and laid her head onto her arms, her eyes closed. She heard the normal night sounds from outside returning. When she listened closely, she heard Brogan's even breathing coming to her from the next room. It was the sound of safety and all that was familiar. She could still feel the love and warmth of Eamon's presence, and she felt like she'd been wrapped up in a safe, warm blanket. She listened to all the sounds around her, but it was the sound of Brogan's breathing that eventually lulled her back to sleep.

Chapter 36

Ella woke to the sight of Brogan standing over her with a big grin.

"It's far too early for you to be this happy!" she said as she sat up and brushed her hair off her face.

"I had a visit last night. He came to me in a dream." Brogan was excited.

"Was it Eamon? He came to me last night as well; Hettie, too. Did he tell you what he wants us to do?"

Brogan smiled. "He did. This isn't bad news, you know. You'll be safer at the home of the Blue Wings, and soon your parents will join us. Now come on, sleepyhead, it's time to get up and face the day. Hettie has a surprise for you. Nothing too exciting, in my estimation, but I think you'll find it most pleasing." Brogan grinned again and then left her alone.

When Ella emerged from her room, she found Hettie and Brogan in the kitchen. It looked like they'd been up for some time. Hettie put her arm around Ella's shoulders and guided her to the door. "I have a surprise for you this morning. I think it'll help you feel much better. Actually, it was Vas who got everything ready." Hettie grabbed her long pole as they went out the door.

Vas was waiting for them by the washroom door. When he saw Ella, he automatically lowered his eyes. Ella swore to herself that she would try to speak to him at some point about his misplaced sense of guilt. She wasn't sure why, but it bothered her that he wouldn't make eye contact.

"All is ready." Vas bowed to both of them and then walked off into the trees.

"Vas has gotten a bath ready for you. He thought perhaps you might enjoy one before breakfast. I find sometimes when I sit in a warm bath, it helps to relax me and make my day just a little nicer. Everything has been prepared, and there's a clean blouse and skirt that I think should fit you. We'll wash your dirty ones tonight. There's a cloak on the stool for you as well."

When Ella walked in, she saw that everything had indeed been laid out for her. The tub was full of water. Soap and towel waited on a small table beside the tub. Clean clothes and a cloak were folded on a stool. She realized right away that the cloak was made from the deer hide Hettie had given Vas to hang yesterday.

"How did you ever find the time to make the cloak?"

"It wasn't me; Vas made it for you, with a little dash of magic from me to help get it ready on time." Hettie laughed. "Vas is very talented, and quite handy, too. I've placed a cloaking spell on the cloak to help you keep a low profile, so to speak." Hettie gave Ella a motherly hug. "Now let me warm up the water so you might have a few moments to relax."

Hettie waved her pole once over the water. She said something so quietly that Ella couldn't make it out. A second later, steam rose from the water. Hettie lifted a small jar and sprinkled its contents into the heated water. A heavenly scent filled the room, unlike anything Ella had ever smelled.

"There; everything's ready. I made the water as warm as I normally have it. If you find it too hot, you can always add cooler water. My only instructions are to take your time and don't worry about anything. When you're ready, come back inside, and I'll have some breakfast ready for you."

Hettie left Ella to her bath. Ella removed her dirty clothes and piled them neatly on the stool next to the clean ones. Slowly she eased herself into the steamy water and felt her entire body begin to relax. This was exactly what she needed; it felt wonderful. She'd have to make a point of thanking Vas for his thoughtfulness.

As she lay there, letting the heat from the water penetrate her muscles, her mind began to wander. This entire situation was more than a little crazy. She reviewed her visit last night with Eamon. Though he'd made her feel loved, some of what he'd said troubled her. How could a select few cause so great a problem? How could her life have changed so much in so short a time?

She felt the most sorry for her parents. Their village was their life. Now they had to leave everything they knew because of fear and stupidity. They were no longer safe around family and friends. It made her incredibly sad.

She wondered if Story Teller would leave the village. For her sake, Ella hoped she would. Their friendship had been commented on in the past, and she believed that, because of their friendship, others might view Story Teller unfavorably. So much anger and unease, caused solely by the color of her wings. It made no sense to her.

Then there was her friendship with Astral. What would come of that? Astral was the only one not to judge her for the color of her wings; she accepted Ella for who she was. She felt bad for not being truthful with her best friend! Perhaps someday she could go to Astral and explain. Maybe, in time, Astral would be willing to come to the Blue Wings' village—if not to live, then at least to visit.

With a start, Ella realized the water had cooled off. How long had she been in there? She must have been lying there for some time. She supposed it was time to get up and out. She would definitely have to thank Vas for his thoughtfulness.

Chapter 37

When Ella emerged from her bath, Brogan was waiting by the door. They entered the main hut and saw Hettie, but Vas wasn't with her. That was too bad; Ella really wanted to thank him.

"Ella, I see the clothes we left for you fit. How did you enjoy your bath?" Hettie was busy cleaning up the kitchen.

Ella's new clothes fit her perfectly. She suspected that this little fact had something to do with Vas. Not only did they fit, but small slits had been sewn into the back of both her shirt and her cloak. The slits would allow her to take her wings out without removing her garments. It was an incredibly thoughtful thing that was often overlooked by others if they themselves were not fairies.

"Yes, the clothes are a perfect fit, and my bath was heavenly, exactly what I needed." Ella gave Hettie a knowing smile and a hug. "Thank you for your thoughtfulness."

"I'm not the only one to have a hand in it." Hettie smiled back.

"Yes, I know. I'll be sure to thank Vas next time I see him."

"You must be hungry! Come, I have breakfast for you on the table."

Ella saw a bowl containing oats, dried fruit, and nuts waiting for her. It was as tasty today as it had been yesterday. Brogan excused himself to go and get himself something to eat.

Once Brogan left, Ella felt it would be a good time to ask Hettie about Vas.

"Hettie, I have a question for you." Hettie stopped what she was doing and looked at Ella. "Do you think it would help if I spoke to Vas about everything? Maybe explain to him he has no reason to feel any guilt toward me? It bothers me that he won't look me in the eye. If anyone has the right to speak to me openly, it's him."

Hettie gently shook her head. "The weight of Vas's guilt is great. I think if you spoke to him about it, it would only make matters worse. He would feel shame for upsetting you and probably make a point of not being around you at all. This is one of those situations when only time itself can heal. He's come a long way, and, in time, you will see that things will get better. Just let this be for now. Vas needs to work through this on his own." Hettie put her hand on Ella's shoulder. "He has great respect for you and would be crushed if he thought he was upsetting you in any way. Give him time, Ella. He'll get over this, you'll see."

Hettie's words made Ella feel a little better.

After Ella ate her morning meal and Brogan returned, Hettie suggested they go to the top of the hill again to talk. It was another beautiful day, far too nice to be inside.

Vas was still nowhere to be seen, but Hettie assured them that he was fine and would be back when he was ready.

The three of them walked up the path and laid out the blanket in the same spot as yesterday. The morning had warmed up enough that they no longer needed to wear their cloaks.

Hettie smiled sadly at Ella. "What I'm about to tell you will be a little difficult for you to believe. I know it to be true and hope you can keep an open mind when you hear what I have to say."

"After all I've been through, I think keeping an open mind will be rather easy in comparison." Ella smiled weakly.

"As you know," Hettie said, "we live in a between world, where all magical creatures should be able to live together harmoniously. That was the intention of its creator. It was to be a place where all magical creatures could live without fear of being persecuted for their abilities. A place where understanding and acceptance would be offered and fear wouldn't have to be part of our existence. Unfortunately, it hasn't worked out that way. Free will was given to all who live here, and that free will has led some to follow a different path. A path paved with hate and fear."

"You said it was the intention of its creator. What creator? I've never heard about any creator in the stories that were told about this world's beginning." Ella looked to Brogan for confirmation.

"You wouldn't have heard about a creator. She wiped out all knowledge of herself." Hettie paused for a moment. "Perhaps it might help if I go back to the beginning. The Creator was disappointed with how her creatures of magic had been behaving. In the fairy world, she knew the Blue Wings were being pressured by the Silver Wings because of their differences. She went to the leader of the Blue Wings and offered to create a world for them that would allow them to live in peace. She permitted a few of the other magical beings to know of its existence. It was hoped that all who lived there would find happiness. It had greatly upset her that the fairy world had become unbalanced and troubled. This was a world the Creator made for those who wanted to live in harmony and peace."

Hettie took a breath. "The Creator was pleased that contentment and harmony prevailed for many centuries. All that changed, however, when the first Silver Wings found the portal from their world to this one. At first, the unease they created was minimal, easily overlooked. The Silver Wings paid homage to the Creator as did the other magical beings, but in time they began to believe the Creator favored the others. Some of their people began to revolt, believing the Blue Wings were partly responsible for setting the Creator against them. I should point out that she had never actually turned her back on the Silver Wings. The problem was that they'd been so used to being the center of all things in their fairy world that they weren't accustomed to sharing favor with others. The Creator believed no creature that dwelled in her land was any greater or better than another. The Silver Wings couldn't understand this way of thinking; they'd been dominant for so long that it was difficult for them to understand the meaning of equality. The Creator waited for things to settle down. It was her hope that, in time, the Silver Wings would accept and understand this new way of living."

Telling this story seemed difficult for Hettie. She stood and started to walk in a circle around Ella and Brogan, making several rounds without saying anything. Before she could speak again, Brogan cleared his throat. "Hettie, if you don't mind, could you not walk in a circle? Pace if you must, but when you circle us like that, you make me dizzy!"

Hettie immediately stopped and sat back down on the blanket. "I'm so sorry. Sometimes when I'm speaking I don't think of my actions."

"Do not worry, my friend. I understand."

"Now, where was I? Oh, yes. Anyway, for a while, things seemed to have worked themselves out. Some tension still existed, but most creatures managed to find ways to live together. When the Silver Wings made their move against the Blue Wings, everything changed. The Creator was so upset over these events that she blamed herself. She believed that if knowledge of her had created this problem, then taking this knowledge away would help to reconnect all beings. She decided to wipe out all memory of herself from those who lived in the between world. She also destroyed all documentation of her existence.

"She learned of Eamon's plan and felt perhaps he was right. With a little time, everything might return to how she'd intended. The problem was, in going to all the other magical beings for their magic, the Silver Wings had caused great pain and distrust. So great was this distrust that, to this day, no other magical being will have contact with the Silver Wings. The Silver Wings' actions effectively destroyed all the harmony that existed among this world's inhabitants."

"I don't understand why the Creator didn't step in and do something to stop the Silver Wings from destroying the Blue Wings. If she is this world's creator, couldn't she have done something?" Ella couldn't understand the actions of this creator.

"She gave all beings free will, and having free will means that someone else can't step in or interfere. You can't place restrictions on free will. Doing so would have gone against all she believed in. All things must be allowed to run their natural course without divine interference. The Creator created all worlds, but it was her hope that in creating this one, things could be different."

Brogan loped to the edge of the hill. When he turned around, he looked directly at Hettie. "I don't mean to sound negative, but if all you say is true, then how is it you know so much about the Creator? If she wiped out all memory of herself, then how is it you know of her and all that happened?"

Chapter 38

"That's a good question, Brogan, and I was about to get to it. You have to understand the shame the Creator felt when the Blue Wings were destroyed. It wasn't unlike that of Vas. She herself had wondered if she could have done anything to prevent the Blue Wings' demise without actually interfering. The truth was, the Creator was very close to the Blue Wings. Not because she favored them, but because they represented all she hoped for in this world. She encouraged the Blue Wings to reach out to the others so any problems among them could be worked out peacefully.

"Unfortunately, the Silver Wings took the Blue Wings' outreach as a sign of aggression. The reason I know of the Creator is that I, too, was close to the Blue Wings. When the Creator found out about Eamon's plans and about you, Ella, she knew, as Eamon did, that you would face great danger and adversity. She and Eamon both hope that you will be the catalyst for the reunion of all magical beings. They hope your existence will help rebuild trust and harmony.

"The Creator has tried to allow her world to heal on its own, but the bad memories haven't faded, and the anger is still strong. This world needs help in healing and reuniting. You're the one who can help; you represent a new beginning. But you can't do this on your own—that's why we're here. When the Creator took herself out of the picture, she allowed my memory of her to stay intact. Why I was chosen, I don't know. I have asked myself that many times. What I am certain of is that you need to know of her, because one day she'll come to you. You need to understand the history in order to understand the future."

"Has the Creator ever spoken to you about what's happening?" Ella kept her voice low. Why, she wasn't sure.

"The Creator came to speak to me shortly after the Blue Wings were destroyed. She told me that when the time was right, she would come to me again. She has come to me twice since. Once she came to let me know of your birth and to say the future looked much brighter." Hettie smiled warmly. "She came again shortly before your fire ceremony. She told me to prepare, because things were going to happen quickly. She wished me luck and asked that I not only help you but also watch out for you. She didn't have to ask that, though, because I'd already decided I would do all I could to assist you."

All three sat on the blanket, thinking. No wonder Hettie had told her to keep an open mind. Ella wished she could tell Hettie she didn't believe her and walk away, but she knew Hettie was telling the truth. She also knew these words would have a huge impact on her life and the lives of everyone around her. It was a lot to take in—it was information overload—and Ella felt overwhelmed again. But she couldn't help going back to one thing.

"From what I've been told," Ella said, "it seems that all the problems in this world and in the fairy world have started at the hands of the Silver Wings. How is it they have been allowed to cause such damage without anyone doing anything to stop it?"

"Ella, I want you to understand something," Hettie said quickly. "Not all Silver Wings are bad. A select few have caused the problems, and there will always be a troublemaking few in any group—that is a guarantee. The problem is, the Silver Wings' select few have made it difficult not to notice them. They stand out far more than any of the others, and their actions have caused the most damage. Fear and distrust can spread like a disease. All it takes is one person—fairy, in this case—to feed on the fear of others. Why the others in their group didn't stand up to them when things started to get out of hand, no one knows. I suspect, once again, it had something to do with fear. But I believe things are different now that others know what can happen. If things were to get out of hand this time, I believe others will intervene. That's my hope, anyway."

Hettie's words didn't comfort Ella. It still came down to the fact that her people, or the people of her parents, were the ones responsible for all the problems. The shame she felt for being a fairy was great. The anger she felt toward her people was even greater! And she knew her own people were coming after her.

Chapter 39

Brogan didn't sleep well that night. Ella knew this because she hadn't slept well, either, and she'd heard him moving around all night. At some point, she drifted off, but not for very long. Her body ached, and her eyelids felt like sandpaper. She pulled the hair off her face, feeling a tangled mess. It would take her forever to brush it out. That was what happened when you tossed and turned all night.

Today was the day she and Brogan were going to the Blue Wings' village. Hettie and Vas would get her parents and possibly Story Teller. Ella prayed with all her heart that Story Teller would agree to leave with her parents. She was sure if Story Teller stayed in the Silver Wings' village, her life would be in danger!

She wouldn't allow herself to think about it right now. She had other things to worry about. She still felt overloaded with all the information she'd been given in such a short amount of time. If anyone shared anything with her today, she was sure her brain would melt.

What she really wanted was to have her parents with her again. Maybe that wasn't really a grown-up way of thinking, but she didn't care. The fact was, she wasn't feeling all that grown up right now.

When Ella came out of her room, she found Brogan sitting beside the fire. Hettie and Vas were nowhere to be seen. Ella found it strange that Hettie had become so important to her in such a short amount of time.

"Where are Hettie and Vas?"

"They went to gather some things for their trip. They're planning to leave right after we do. Hettie wants me to remind you to connect with your parents as soon as possible so they can be ready to go. Perhaps you should eat first. I suspect you'll need the extra strength to deal with your mother." Brogan gave a half-hearted smirk to show he was joking.

The problem was, she knew his words weren't far from the truth. It was going to take all her patience to get through that conversation. Maybe she'd try to connect with her father instead. Let him deal with her mother.

Ella sat at her usual spot at the table. Beside her plate were a fresh loaf of homemade bread and a jar of jellied fruit. The smell of the bread penetrated her sleepy, foggy mind, and her stomach growled. There was only one downfall about having Hettie around: with all the good food being served, she'd soon be too fat to fly.

Ella ate and then went outside to clean up. After untangling her hair—leaving what felt like several bald spots in the process—she went back inside to see if Hettie and Vas had returned. They hadn't.

She decided to go to her room and connect with her father. It would be far easier to speak to him than to her mother. He would have all the same questions, but he would be willing to wait for an explanation. He would also be far more discreet when talking with her.

She made the connection with her father right away and gave him a short version of what was going on. She told him Hettie and Vas would come to get them in two days. To her father's credit, he didn't ask a hundred questions when she mentioned Vas, who was completely unknown to him. He promised he would speak to

Story Teller and impress upon her the importance of her leaving with them. Ella knew if anyone could convince Story Teller to go, it was him. They broke the connection after she promised him all was well with her and reassured him that they would see each other soon. That was a lot easier than trying to explain it all to her mother. She wasn't under any delusions, though; she knew she'd be in big trouble when she saw her mother later for connecting with her father and not her!

When she returned to the main room, Hettie and Vas were waiting. "How did the conversation with your mother go?" Hettie asked.

"I didn't speak with her; I spoke with my father, instead. He'll make sure they're ready, but we don't know if Story Teller will be with them or not. I guess you'll know when you get there. Is everything ready?"

"Everything's ready. I put together some food for you to take. It's in the basket you came here with. Your extra clothes are in there as well. This should tide you over until we all get there. If you start to run short on food, I'm sure Brogan can stir something up for you. Don't worry, sweetheart. Everything will be fine, and we'll see you very soon." Hettie hugged Ella. They stood that way for several moments before Hettie let go. "You and Brogan should be on your way. Vas and I will leave after you've gone. I want you to connect with me as soon as you get there so I know you arrived safely. Once I hear from you, we'll leave." Hettie looked at Vas, who nodded.

"Well, I guess I'll speak to you in a moment." Ella tried to be upbeat, but the words came out shaky and uncertain. "Are you ready?" she asked Brogan. Brogan nodded. She picked up the basket and then put her arms around his neck, just like Eamon had told her to. "Here we go," she said.

Chapter 40

"Wait! Hold on for a second," Hettie called out. Brogan glanced at Hettie and then looked back at Ella. Tears were streaming down her face. "What's the matter, little one?"

"Nothing, everything, I don't really know. I guess I'm scared. We don't know what'll happen when we leave here." Ella tried to wipe the tears from her face, but more kept coming.

Hettie gave Ella another hug. "Everything will work out. We'll be with you again in a few days."

"Why can't you use your magic to bring my parents to the Blue Wings' village, the way you did with us in the forest? That way, you could come with us now."

"I can't. I used a spell to transport you and Brogan, and I used the last two key ingredients getting you here. Vas looked for the plants I need, but he was able to find only one. I need both for my spell to work. I'm sorry, Ella, but we must travel to get your parents."

"I'm going to be with you," Brogan reminded her. "Everything will work out; you'll see."

"We didn't think anything would happen on the way here, but it did. We don't know what will happen," Ella said.

"Remember, you're now aware of all your abilities and have additional ways of defending yourself. You must have confidence in yourself," Hettie said.

"You're right, of course. I'm just being silly." Ella wiped the tears from her eyes again and took a big breath. "I'm sorry for my meltdown. Let me wash my face, and then we'll leave."

Hettie smiled. "That sounds like a good idea. You don't need to be sorry, Ella. What happened to you on the way here gives you the right to feel scared."

"I guess." Ella bowed her head and left to clean up.

After washing her face and calming herself down, Ella returned to the others. She picked up the basket again and looked at Hettie.

"Please take extra care with my parents. Perhaps if Story Teller decides not to come you could go to her and explain why it's so important."

"I'll see what I can do, sweetheart."

Suddenly, a huge booming sound erupted. The vibrations shook the entire cave; Ella felt the tremors going up her legs. Before anyone had time to react, another crashing boom erupted, much closer this time. Things toppled off the tables and shelves. Dust and debris fell from the ceiling, and they could hear some of the trees outside falling to the ground.

"What's going on?" Ella moved to the center of the room to avoid having something fall on her. Panic set in.

"We're under attack." Hettie's words were edged with anger.

"How can that be? I would have sensed if someone was near. We all would have. Plus, your home is cloaked!" She tried to reach out with her mind to see if she could sense anyone, but she felt nothing.

There was another explosive boom. This time, when the ground shook, a crack started forming beneath their feet. Pieces of the hill starting falling in on them.

"It's a magical attack. From whom, I don't know, but it's strong magic and whoever's responsible means business." Another boom, a little farther away this time.

"Ella, you and Brogan must leave immediately! Vas and I will go as soon as you do. Go quickly; I'm not sure how much stress my little cave can take before it falls in."

"What about you guys? How'll you get out of here safely? You should come with us for now!"

Hettie ran to the door and grabbed her magical pole. "We'll be fine, I promise you. I can look after us, but you must go now. I'll see you soon." Hettie strode toward Vas. "Connect with me in an hour. *Go now!*" She had to scream to be heard over the falling rock and debris.

There was another loud explosion, which sounded like it had landed directly over them. Parts of the ceiling started falling down in chunks. A giant piece of rock missed Ella by a fraction of an inch. Still holding onto the basket with one hand, she picked up her skirt and took three bounding leaps to Brogan. Only when she reached him did she realize something was wrong. Brogan was lying on the floor, with something dark spreading out under his head.

"*Oh, no! No, no, this can't be! Brogan's been hurt!*" Ella screamed as loudly as she could. The noise around them had become almost deafening. Her heart was hammering so hard she thought it would hammer right out of her chest.

"Get him out of here! You can help him after. Ella, get out of here, *now!*" Right after Hettie screamed this, a terrible ripping sound came from above them. The trees were falling, and the roots were being torn from the ground.

Ella kneeled down. Pushing the basket up to her elbow, she wrapped her arms around Brogan's neck. Another loud crack came from directly above her. Without thinking, she lifted her arm and felt energy flow out of her hand.

Chapter 41

Energy flowed from her body and out through her hand. When she looked up, she saw a barrier of energy surrounding her and Brogan. Seconds after the barrier was erected, a giant piece of rock crashed down on top of it. When it hit, Ella heard a strange buzzing noise, and multicolored sparks shot out. She automatically covered Brogan's head with her free arm, but the rock hadn't penetrated the barrier. Outside the barrier on the ground beside them was a giant piece of rock with dirt and tree roots sticking out of it. The side of the rock that had hit the barrier had melted slightly, and the roots had started to smolder.

Looking back down at Brogan, Ella realized she'd lowered her arm to protect him. She quickly looked up; to her relief, the force field remained. She wasn't sure how that worked, but she didn't care. She was just happy to see the barrier. Without the use of both her arms, she wasn't sure how she'd get them out. More of the ceiling was starting to fall. The crack in the floor was growing much larger. She scanned the room, looking for Hettie and Vas, but they were gone. She prayed they'd gotten out safely and were still able to get away.

Ella wrapped her arms around Brogan's neck. She bent over him and closed her eyes. She took a deep breath and let the image of the Blue Wings' village that Eamon had shown her earlier take shape in her mind's eye. Then she allowed these words to flow through the image: "I want to be here!"

An electric burst of energy flowed through her body, starting in her tummy and moving outward from there. She felt the energy transferring between her and Brogan, slowly at first, but then quickly picking up momentum. A loud humming sound filled her head, and she felt a warm rush of air. A buzzing of electrical currents passed all around them, the humming got much louder, and Ella felt like they were falling from somewhere very high. All the hair on her body stood straight up. Her entire body felt fuzzy, her head dizzy. Her stomach pitched and rolled. Just when she thought she was going to get sick, the sensations stopped. She felt all the energy that had been madly swirling around them slowly being pulled back into her. When she opened her eyes, they were sitting on the ground. They were no longer in Hettie's hut. They were in the middle of the Blue Wings' village.

The first thing Ella felt was the heat coming off her amulet. She could feel the pain starting as the amulet got warmer. Quickly she unlocked her arms from around Brogan's neck and put the basket down beside them. When she turned back to Brogan, she saw her arm. The arm that had been beneath him was now completely covered in his blood. Carefully, she looked over his head and neck to see where all the blood was coming from. There was a very large gash just to the side of his left ear. One of the falling rocks must have hit him and knocked him unconscious. Her heart started to pound when she realized she couldn't feel him breathing.

The panic at that moment was almost overwhelming. Tears streamed down her face, but she had no time to wipe them away. It took a moment for her brain to kick in and make her body move. She gently laid her hand on the side of his chest. She wanted to feel it moving; if it was, it meant he was still alive. She held her hand there for several seconds but couldn't feel anything. She moved her hand a little lower, holding it there for several more seconds. She was just about to try the other side when she felt the faint rise of his chest. She sighed with relief.

The pain from the amulet was getting stronger, but she had to ignore it; she didn't have time. Placing both her hands over the gash on Brogan's head, she let all her remaining energy flow through her hands and into the wound. Her concern now was how much blood he'd already lost and was still losing, but then the flow of blood lessened, and the edges of the wound started to stitch together.

The longer she held her hands over the wound, the weaker she felt. She'd already used up so much energy creating the force field and transporting them here. The amulet wasn't able to keep up with the increased demand. She felt herself becoming lightheaded, and her arms started to shake. Darkness crept in at the edges of her mind, and her vision blurred. If she didn't rest, she was going to faint. She quickly pulled back her hands, slumping forward. She didn't even have the energy to sit up. Brogan's wound was still open and bleeding, and a feeling of helplessness washed over her. She needed her energy restored before she could help him further. Brogan's life essence was leaving him; she could feel it. Brogan didn't have time for her energy to return. He needed help now, or he would die.

Carefully she leaned over and gently lifted his head into her lap. "Brogan, I'm so sorry! Please don't leave me. Wait for a while; I can help, but we have to wait. Just hold on for a bit longer, okay? Please; you have to wait." Ella sobbed the words. She was so drained and tired that she could do nothing but cry.

As she held Brogan, she remembered Hettie's words about the Creator. If ever there was a time to pray to her, this was it. Ella lifted her head, which was an effort in itself, and looked at the sky. "Please, Creator, help me. If you do exist, then please, I need your help. I need your help to make him better. He's my family, and I'm not ready to lose him. So please, please help me." Her words got quieter and quieter. She was so tired that speaking was becoming difficult. She waited for a few seconds, but nothing happened.

What had she expected? It felt like part of her heart was being ripped out of her chest. She was completely helpless and totally alone. She leaned over Brogan again and let her tears fall. Some of her tears fell into Brogan's wound. Just as the last tear landed, a flash of blue light streamed up from the gash, almost blinding her.

She was infused with an electrical charge that wasn't coming from the amulet. It didn't matter where it came from, as long as she had the energy to heal Brogan! When she went to put her hand over Brogan's wound, she saw that it was already healing. It was almost completely closed, and the bleeding had stopped. She watched in awe as the wound quickly stitched itself back together and the fur around it started to grow back. It was the most amazing thing she'd ever seen.

She was about to check Brogan again when she heard a strange noise up ahead. *No*, she thought, *no more problems. I can't deal with anything else right now.*

Chapter 42

Ella saw a bright flash of light—and then she saw her. Several yards away stood a woman dressed completely in white. Her cloak covered her from head to toe. The hood obscured her face, but Ella already knew who she was. A giant circle of light surrounded the Creator, and it seemed the light was actually coming from within the Creator herself. The glow got closer and closer. When it finally touched them, Ella felt warmth and love emanating from it.

"Ella, Princess of the Blue Wings, leader of Clan Hope. My child." The voice of the Creator was soft and melodious, like an orchestra of several voices mixed together. Ella didn't hear it so much as feel it. All the strain, tension, and fear from the last few moments slid away.

"My child, rise up before me. Stand tall and stand strong." Ella was stunned. Not knowing what else to do, she carefully lowered Brogan's head and stood. She felt her wings come out, and she could tell from the blue glow around her that they were blazing brightly. She took several steps toward the Creator. The closer she got, the brighter her wings seemed to get.

The Creator, seeming to glide forward, soon stood before Ella. The Creator's hood was actually a sheer veil that was an extension of her hair. She put her hands on Ella's shoulders.

"You've done well and learned much in a very short time. The wheels of your destiny have already begun to turn, and time will be something you won't have in abundance. It's time, my child, to call to your people and gather them here with you. Only with the strength of unity can you fight the hate and fear that stand against you."

Ella felt an incredible warmth pass from the Creator to her.

"I have given you a gift—a gift of unending power. Never again will you find yourself drained and unable to help. You must remember that with this gift comes great responsibility. If you use this gift for harm, or for any reason that isn't for the greater good, I will strip you of this gift, and it will never be returned. I give this gift to you because, as you believe in me, I, too, believe in you. There will be a time when temptation calls to you, but never allow fear or anger to determine how you use your power. Even in the darkest moments, and those moments are sure to come, don't let the darker side of yourself overpower what you know is right. I believe the path you walk is the path that will lead to great changes. I believe the love you hold in your heart will help heal the hearts of so many. If you continue on as you have, I believe peace and love will prevail."

The Creator dropped her hands and glided back a few steps. It looked like she was going to leave, so Ella quickly spoke. "Why couldn't you help change things before? Why did what happened today have to happen at all? You're our creator. Help me understand."

"All things happen for a reason. We may not know what those reasons are or understand them, but there's a reason all the same. It's not my place to alter destiny. My interference could be detrimental on many levels. I am the Creator. All magical beings are my children. Some of my children have done well, and some struggle. Whatever my children have become, they are still my children. They must live to learn, make mistakes to move forward, and live with the outcomes of their decisions. We never stop learning, and each day brings a new lesson. What happened today was tragic."

The Creator lowered her head and turned her back to Ella. "All those years ago, when the Silver Wings went to the other magical beings to gain extra magic, they received far more than they needed. One of the male Silver Wings realized they had an abundance of power, far more than what they needed to conquer the Blue Wings. Without the others' knowledge, he hid that extra magic. He hoped to one day use it for his own benefit, to further his personal status. After the Blue Wings were destroyed, the uprising of his people destroyed any hope of his ascending the political ranks. This magic sat undisturbed for all these years. Magic is, as you know, amazing in several ways. The unique quality of magic is that in time, if it is not used, it will gather within itself more strength and power. The ancestors of the hoarding fairy were eventually told of this hidden magic. They agreed it could be a great danger to them were any of the others to find out, so they agreed to keep the magic hidden—until today. With your increasing strength, their fear of you grows. They fear your strength and your potential!" As the Creator said this, she turned back toward Ella.

"With their fear comes the inability to make sound decisions. They used some of the magic today, against you. You should know that not all the hoarded magic was used. Some remains to be used against you at a future time.

"Only a few have allowed their fears to overcome them. Many more now would defend you and do not wish you harm. This is a huge step for them. With this step comes hope that many more will see you for who you truly are. Hope."

Ella was speechless. She wasn't sure she wanted to be anyone's hope; and, after today, she felt the opposite of hopeful. "It takes only a few to spread fear and gather others to their cause. With each day that passes, there are more fairies who wish to destroy me! Where is all this hope? How do I conquer that?"

"You conquer it with love. There are not as many against you as there are for you. You forget—other magical beings are willing to stand beside you. You do not stand against these few alone. Love, understanding and forgiveness will go a long way in helping you."

The Creator glided closer to Ella and took one of her hands into both of hers. Ella could feel the light that surrounded the Creator spill into her. "You will never fight alone nor stand alone. Call to your people Ella, they need you as much as you need them." With those last words the Creator let go of Ella's hand and was gone.

Chapter 43

Ella stared at the space the Creator had, just a moment ago, been standing. This entire situation was feeling a little surreal. When Hettie told her about the Creator, she had some doubts. Now she just felt ridiculous for even questioning her existence. This day was going to change everything she'd ever believed in. The Creator was real! For the first time in a very long time, Ella felt there really was hope.

The Creator said she'd given her a gift. Now that everything had calmed down, Ella could feel her whole body tingling with renewed energy. At that moment, she remembered Brogan. How could she have forgotten him? She ran to his side and heard him groan. Kneeling down, Ella lifted his head back onto her lap. She looked for the gash on his head, but it was gone. This time, when she placed her hand on his side, there was no mistaking the strong thud of his heart or the steady intake of breath. He was going to be all right! The rush of relief was intense.

"Brogan, can you hear me? I need you to wake up." Ella's voice was shaky.

Brogan's eyes fluttered open, and he quickly closed them again. "Oh, my head! It feels like little explosions are going off inside it." His voice was weak and quiet, but it came out clear.

"Oh, Brogan, you don't know how scared I was! I thought I lost you!" She laid her head on Brogan's, crying with relief.

After a while, Brogan spoke again. "Hettie and Vas, did they manage to get out? Have you spoken to Hettie yet?"

"Hettie! In all the confusion, I forgot. I think they got out, but I'm not sure. Give me a moment to connect with her."

Ella lifted her head and closed her eyes. She got a solid picture of Hettie in her mind and started to mentally reach out to her. It took only seconds for her mind to connect.

"Ella! Oh, thank the Creator you're all right! How's Brogan?"

"Brogan's doing much better now, though we came very close to losing him. I'll tell you everything when you get here. Vas is with you, and you're both safe?"

"He is, and we're fine. We're on our way to get your parents and should be there tomorrow. From their village to yours is a little less than a day's travel. We'll see you in two days' time. You will be safe in your village, but, whatever you do, don't leave until we get there."

"We won't be going anywhere. Brogan's going to need a few days to regain his strength. We'll watch for you in two days' time. Take care, and be safe!"

Ella broke the connection and looked down at Brogan. "They are both safe and on their way to my parents."

Brogan nodded faintly. The movement must have caused him pain, because he let out another moan.

"Your head pains you greatly. Perhaps I can help with that." Ella placed her hands on either side of Brogan's large head. She willed her hands to send healing strength in so he wouldn't feel any more pain. She heard Brogan take a sharp breath and felt his entire body tense. She was about to let go when his body relaxed and his breathing evened out. She waited until she could feel the power in her hands lessen, signaling the end of the energy transfer. "How's your pain now? Has it lessened any?"

Brogan slowly opened his eyes and lifted his head a little. He stopped, waited, and then smiled. "Yes, the pain's receded. Thank you." Brogan shifted his body weight so he could sit up. Then he lowered his head and closed his eyes again.

"What is it? Has your pain returned?" Ella moved to put her hands on his head again.

"No, it's not the pain. I'm just feeling really dizzy. Give me a moment; the feeling is starting to pass."

"It's because you lost so much blood. The wound has healed, but your body needs time. You need to rest. Wait here, and I'll look for a place where you can lie down for a while."

"You shouldn't wander alone. We don't even know where we are. Give me a second, and we'll go together."

For the first time, Ella looked at her surroundings. What she saw took her breath away. They were indeed at the Blue Wings' village. It was similar to the village she'd grown up in, but at the same time completely different. The village was beautiful in a natural, peaceful way. The stories she'd heard didn't do it justice!

The trees here were the largest Ella had ever seen. The tree huts seemed a little larger than the ones from her parents' village, but that wasn't what made them so different. These tree huts weren't built into or around the trees but seemed to be grown by the trees, actually part of them. The trunks of the trees were wide and hollow, allowing for the main structure of the house, and each house sat at the top of the tree, just before the smaller branches started to grow out. The small branches above the house reached down and wove together, creating the roof. The leaves overlapped like green shingles, making the roof watertight. Lower branches wove around the house, creating a small veranda that included a leaf railing.

Only one part of each house didn't seem to be part of the tree itself. On the side of each tree where the trunk was thickest and sturdiest stood large round rocks, one on top of the other, to create what must be the fireplace. Ella could see that the top of each rock column leaned slightly out, allowing smoke to move away from the tree. The walls of the house were rather thick, and there were several small windows in different shapes and sizes. Some of the houses had only one floor, but several had two floors, like her parents' house. The exteriors of the houses were covered in bark, rather than being stained a color. The trees were spaced out evenly and allowed room between them for fairies to fly. Paths made of soft, spongy moss ran through the village. It was amazing to see!

Scanning the village, she could see that the village bower wasn't far from where they stood, but she wasn't able to see it clearly through the trees. If she couldn't see it clearly, then she couldn't transport them. They would have to walk.

She caught a movement from the corner of her eye. Quickly turning around, she saw that Brogan had gotten to his feet but was swaying badly, close to falling. "Brogan! What are you doing?" When Ella was looking around, she'd taken several steps away from him. She quickly ran back to his side and steadied him. "You're going to be very weak for a day or two. Why must you be so stubborn? We're in the Blue Wings' village. We're safe now."

Brogan gave her a dirty look. She knew it would be futile to argue with him, and she was too happy he was alive to want to argue anyway. "The village bower is just over there. We'll go there for now, because it's the only dwelling built on the ground. We'll walk slowly."

Brogan bowed his head in agreement. Ella could see that just standing was taking all his energy. She wasn't sure how they were going to get to the bower. "Brogan, you don't look so good. Are you sure you're all right? We can stay here for a while if you need to."

"I've never in all my life felt this weak! I feel like a newborn pup. But if we go slowly, I should be fine."

It took them quite a while to reach the bower. They had to stop several times for Brogan to rest. Ella could see his entire body shaking with fatigue.

Traveling slowly allowed Ella to take in the details of the bower. She was stunned to see that the bower had also been grown, not built. Smaller trees had woven themselves tightly together and developed up, creating walls and the roof. The leaves of the trees covered the entire building.

Finally arriving at the bower, Ella opened the door. The doorknob was a large growth from one of the trees. When the door opened, smaller branches that could bend attached the door to the wall. It took a moment for their eyes to adjust to the dimness. Ella could smell the familiar smells of a bower. She had a sense of well being and knew she was home!

"We'll go to the fire pit, and you can rest there. I'll start a fire for us and find some blankets to make you a pallet. We can stay here tonight."

Walking toward the pit of the eternal flame, Ella saw round rocks similar to those of the tree hut chimneys surrounding the pit. The floor of the bower was covered in the same soft, spongy moss as the paths outside. Ella looked at the fire pit and realized there probably hadn't been a fire in it for hundreds of years. Not since her ancestors' demise.

They were only steps away from the fire pit when a loud whooshing sound startled them. The sound started off loud and continued to get louder, and Ella felt a breeze rush past. Without thinking, she pushed Brogan to the ground and covered him with her body. Terror seized her; her heart was beating overtime. She didn't know how, but their attackers had managed to follow them from Hettie's! With Brogan still so weak, she had no idea what she should do.

Chapter 44

The room seemed to amplify the wind and sounds. Brogan was yelling something to her, but she couldn't hear him over the noise. Suddenly, as quickly as it had started, everything became quiet. Brogan was still yelling at her when the silence fell. ". . . if you don't get off me! Ella, let me up *now!*" His booming voice echoed off the walls, jarring in the sudden silence. Ella lifted herself off of him and sat down.

They looked at each other. Just as she was about to ask Brogan what happened, a loud crackling erupted from the fire pit. A blazing fire danced in the center. The entire bower immediately filled with warmth. All Ella could do was stare in wonder with her mouth wide open.

"After all we've been through, this is what shocks you?" Brogan was looking at the fire and smiling. Relief coursed through Ella. She leaned on her hands and let her head fall back, and then she started to laugh. Brogan laughed, too. It felt good to laugh after all they'd been through!

"I thought we were under attack again," she said though bursts of giggles.

"So did I." Brogan's laughter started to die down.

Ella looked over and saw he was having a hard time keeping his eyes open. That ended her laughter rather quickly. Everything was starting to catch up with him, and his body demanded rest. They scooted closer to the fire and sat there for a while, enjoying the peace and quiet.

"I must get some sleep. Don't wander far, Ella. Maybe you should try to get some rest as well." With those words, Brogan fell fast asleep.

Brogan wasn't sure how long he slept, but when he awoke, he definitely felt a little better. He wasn't feeling one hundred percent, and he still felt weak, but at least it was an improvement. When he lifted his head, he found that Ella had moved him, more like dragged him, onto a pallet of blankets and was now snuggled up behind him with her arm wrapped around his neck. When he lifted his head, her arm dropped down, and she began to stir. His heart swelled with love. Not that he would ever admit it to anyone, especially her, but he couldn't help but reflect on all she'd done for him and all she was willing to do. He also realized that what he would do for her was no longer done out of a sense of duty. She was his family, and you always protect your family. Her small voice broke through his thoughts.

"Brogan, are you awake?"

"I am." His voice was husky. Hopefully she would think it was from just having woken up.

"How do you feel?"

"Much better. I still feel a little weak, but that should pass. I probably need something to eat."

"I thought as much. I have some food for you. Wait here, and I'll get it."

Ella jumped up and went to the door leading outside. When she opened it, sunlight streamed in. Just as quickly as the sunlight had entered, it was blocked again, and Brogan could see Ella walking back. When she got to his side, he saw she held some raw meat.

"Where did you get that?"

"I knew you'd need something, so I asked the Creator for help. She sent me several small animals that were willing to give their lives so you might get stronger. There's one wild boar and two rabbits."

"What do you mean, you asked the Creator?"

"With all that happened, I forgot to tell you. Here, eat while I tell you."

Ella told Brogan what happened from the time of their transportation to the Blue Wings' village right up to the point of him waking. "You woke up moments after the Creator left. If it hadn't been for her, I believe you wouldn't be here now." Tears filled her eyes when she thought about how close she'd come to losing him.

"She's real! I wasn't sure I believed Hettie. I knew Hettie believed it, but I questioned the truth of this creator's existence. You actually saw her?"

"I did. To be more accurate, I saw a woman in a long white cloak with a veil. I never did see her face or any other part of her body. Even when she put her hands on my shoulders or took my hand, the sleeves of her cloak covered them. When I was with her, I didn't have time to think about it; but now that I'm explaining it, it sounds rather strange. She could walk up to me and I wouldn't know it was her."

"I seriously doubt you wouldn't know it was her if she walked up to you." Brogan gave her his lopsided grin.

"Well, you must be feeling better, smarty pants." Ella giggled. "Anyway, you know what I mean."

"Just so you know, I have never worn pants in my life, never mind smart ones." Brogan said this with such a straight face that Ella had no choice but to laugh.

"Yep, you're definitely feeling better." Ella stood and stretched. "Is there anything else you need?"

"I don't think so, although I could get used to having you serve me and take care of me. I'll have to get hurt more often!"

"Oh, you're a funny guy, mister warrior. Your days of getting taken care of are almost over. Hettie will be here with my parents tomorrow, so I have to make sure everything's ready. There are some tree huts nearby that I think will be perfect for them. Hettie may need some kind of ladder or steps to get up to hers, though. Hmmm. I never considered that until now. Well, I'm sure one of us can fly her up for the first few days until something can be made. My father will come up with something. I'm not sure where Vas will want to stay . . ."

"Ella, *Ella*!" Brogan had been trying to get her attention for a while. Finally Ella heard him and stopped talking.

"What?"

"What do you mean, they'll be here tomorrow? It'll take them two days; they won't be here until the day after. Don't you remember Hettie telling you this?"

"Brogan, tomorrow will be two days. You've been asleep for a day and a half now."

"What? What are you talking about? I only slept for a few hours."

"No, Brogan, you fell asleep early yesterday. You slept through the entire day yesterday, all of the night, and all of this morning. You were very weak, and your body needed the rest. You have no idea how much blood you lost." Ella sat back down and put her hand on Brogan's shoulder for reassurance. It was nice to be the one giving the reassurance for a change.

"Why didn't you wake me?" His annoyance was clear.

"I just told you. You were very weak, and you needed to rest. You wouldn't have slept that long if you didn't need to. Don't worry; I didn't leave the village. I only walked around to check it out and to see where everything is."

"You shouldn't have done that alone." Brogan softened his tone of voice. "Since you have, and all is well, I guess there was no harm done. How bad does the village look? After all these years, it must need some work."

"Well, that's the strange part."

Chapter 45

Brogan raised his head to look at Ella. "What do you mean, strange? Is it something I need to worry about?"

"No, not strange in that way. I mean strange as in the condition of the village. It doesn't seem like this village was ever deserted, never mind for centuries. In fact, it seems like the fairies who lived here just recently left. The village is set up like any other fairy village. There's the village bower, which we're in, and the tree huts within the village. When I walked through it, I felt like I was in my parents' village." Ella couldn't bring herself to call that village hers. It was no longer home. This was home.

"Things are different here, Ella. This bower and the tree huts are all different. I'm not sure I understand what you mean, but it sounds like everything is good."

"That's what's so strange. You would think, after all these years of having no one living here, that certain natural occurrences would have happened. The forest should have started to resume its rightful place, growing around the paths, the tree huts, and any other area the Blue Wings altered. The tree huts should have changed, especially because they seem to have been grown from the trees! The forest animals would have come in, seeking shelter, and what better shelter is there than an empty tree hut? Look around us—look at this bower—it doesn't look like it's been deserted for years. The moss on the ground hasn't overgrown or died. Even the fire pit looks like the fire never went out. It just doesn't look like it should after being abandoned for centuries. It's almost like a blanket of protection was laid on top of the village. Everything is in pristine condition. That's what I mean by strange."

"Do you remember the day I first came to your village? Story Teller told you about the one Silver Wing fairy who stumbled upon the Blue Wings' village. Even then, this village hadn't been used for a century or more. But when he found the village, he said it looked like the fairies who lived here had only just left. This village was protected, waiting for its people to return. That time has finally arrived. Its people are returning, you being the first of many. I'm not sure what protection spell was used, but it was placed on the village not only to keep others from finding it but also to keep it safe until you were ready to come home."

"Well, I have a question. If there was a protection spell placed on the village, how did that one fairy manage to stumble across it?"

"No one knows. I do know that the same fairy, after his return from this village, was asked to guide others back here. He'd been here once; he should have been able to find it again; but he couldn't. Some believed it was because he had others with him, so he tried again on his own. He wandered for days before he gave up. He never did find the village again."

"How strange. A village this size, although not big by fairy standards, is still large enough not to be missed. How's it possible that he stumbled upon it once but wasn't able to again?" Ella spoke more to herself than to Brogan. Brogan answered anyway.

"No one's sure, but I have my own theory. I believe he was guided here by some unseen force. He was needed. Someone had to find the village in order to find the journals."

Brogan stopped to let Ella think about what he'd just said. "What did those journals contain? Information on what happened to the Blue Wings and, of course, the prophesy. I believe he was sent here to find the journals. Once the journals were found, however, there was no other reason for him or any others to come back. The Blue Wings wanted to keep the village safe for their own to return." Brogan watched Ella's face as she digested this.

"This would make sense, actually. I wouldn't have thought of that. In fact, I'd forgotten about his finding some of Eamon's journals."

"I just thought of something. Didn't you say the Creator told you that now was the time for you to call your people?" Ella nodded. "Have you called to them yet?"

"I did a couple of times already. I'm not sure if I'm doing it right. I've never done anything like it before. It's not like connecting with another individual. I'm casting out a call to many, and I'm not even sure where they are. I'll have to remember to ask Hettie about it tomorrow; maybe she'll know more. Anyway, if I did do it correctly, then other Blue Wings should begin to arrive soon. I sure hope they can find the village."

"Don't worry; they'll find the village. The village isn't shielded against its own kind. I'm also sure they heard you."

Ella said nothing. Brogan stood and looked down at Ella. "Let's go for a walk. I feel like I need to move around a little. This will give me a chance to get familiar with the village."

Ella gave him a dirty look. "You shouldn't do too much; you're still weak. You need to rest more. There will be enough time in the morning to look around."

"Ella, if it were up to you, I wouldn't move at all for several more days. It's not in me to just sit around. I need to move a little; it'll do me good. If I start to get tired, I promise you, you'll be the first to know. By the way, how did you move me? Where I woke was not where I fell asleep."

Ella knew there was no point in arguing with him about moving around. Brogan was too stubborn for his own good. "The Creator helped me. I'll agree to this walk only if it's a short one, and then we'll come back here so you can rest more."

Brogan growled deeply. "Fine. But remember, little one, your days of telling me what to do are almost at an end."

With that, Brogan turned toward the door and started walking. He didn't even look back to see if she was following. He knew she would be.

Chapter 46

Ella spent part of the evening and all the next morning cleaning and washing. She cleaned up four of the tree huts for her parents and Hettie. She washed everything down in the tree hut and took the dirty bedding to the river to wash. The river wasn't all that large, but it ran right through the back half of the village. She even managed to wash her soiled dress! It took several washings to get all the blood out.

She hung the wet bedding on a line she found not far from the river that was tied to two trees. She was sure this was the original purpose of the line. Then she found clean linen to put on the stripped beds. The bed frames looked like they had grown from the trees as well. The mattresses were made from vines woven together, and each was covered with a cloth bag stuffed with what looked like bull rush seeds. It was very interesting to see how different the Blue Wings and the Silver Wings were from one another in the way they set up their villages.

It was amazing to her that the blankets were still so clean after all these years; but she did let the clean blankets hang on the line for a while to air them out. When she pulled the blankets out, she found that some had intricate pictures woven into them. The Silver Wings wove different colors into their blankets, but never pictures. The detail of each picture was astounding, and the colors were brighter than anything Ella had ever seen. She wondered what the weavers had used as dye. After all these years, they still seemed as bright as the day they'd been made. She had just hung up the last blanket when she heard Brogan call.

"I'm over here." She was walking back to the river to check on the wet bedding. It'd been a wonderfully warm, sunny morning, so it wouldn't take long for it to dry. She turned around and saw Brogan meandering toward her.

"Are you still cleaning? You know, princesses don't normally do all this menial work." Brogan's tone was sarcastic. He stopped right in front of her. Ella could see the smirk on his face.

"I'm still the same fairy I was before. Besides, if I don't do the cleaning, who will? You?" Ella put her hands on her hips. Her wings were out, because the sun felt good on them. It had been so long since she was able to just have them out without worry. There definitely were some advantages to being here.

"I'm no maid. Besides, you wouldn't like my idea of clean." Ella smiled at the look on Brogan's face as he thought of cleaning.

"My point exactly! Feeling better today?"

"I feel much better. I don't think I'd be able to run any distances, but at least I don't feel weak and useless. Are you almost done? They'll be here soon!" Brogan looked around.

"I've done as much as I'm going to do. All I need to do now is put away this clean bedding when it dries, and it's almost dry already. When do you think they'll get here?"

"It depends on when they left your parents' village, how easy it's been for them to travel, and how many stops they've made. I'm sure they'll be walking, because I don't think Hettie will allow them to fly. Do you think Story Teller will be with them?"

"I honestly don't know. I don't think she'll be safe if she stays. My father was going to speak to her, and he can be very persuasive when he needs to be. I just pray she's with them."

Ella had been worrying all morning about Story Teller's decision. She'd also been worrying about her mother's attitude toward Hettie. Even though her mother hadn't met Hettie, she was distrustful of her. Ella hoped her mother wouldn't show her distrust in an overt or rude way. She knew her father would be the voice of reason, but her mother didn't always listen to him. Then there was Vas. How would her parents take to him? Even though Vas had good intentions, he still came across as a little strange.

Ella felt like a parent worrying over her child's behavior. How bizarre that the roles were reversed.

When Ella emerged from her thoughts, she realized Brogan had wandered over to a group of trees to lie in the shade. He didn't fool her; she knew he was pretending to rest so she wouldn't put him to work. Ignoring him, she continued to check the bedding, which still hung on the line. She neatly folded everything that was dry and spread out everything that was still damp.

"Brogan, I'm going to take these blankets up to the tree huts and put them away. I won't be long. When I'm done, we can go back to the bower and have a light lunch. I have another rabbit for you from yesterday." When she spoke, Brogan lifted his head from his front paws. The only indication he gave of hearing her was a slight nod.

Brogan and Ella sat outside the village bower by the outdoor fire pit. It was far too nice for them to sit inside. Ella finished what was left in the basket Hettie had sent with them. If they didn't get here soon, she'd have to go hunt something up later to eat. She'd noticed some small fruit bushes just on the other side of the river, but she didn't want to leave until everyone arrived.

Brogan had dozed off again. He sure was sleeping a lot, which worried her. She'd have to ask her mother if any herbs could help restore his energy. At least she *could* worry about him. It still upset her when she thought of how close she'd come to losing him. She slid over a little to sit closer to Brogan. She needed to have him close just for a little reassurance.

The two of them sat there for part of the afternoon. It was nice to just sit and feel the sun shining down on them. A breeze had blown in, making the temperature just right. Ella was starting to wonder if she should connect with someone to find out where they were when she felt the stirrings of sensation start to form. Someone was coming. Brogan must have felt it, too, because he lifted his head.

"Someone approaches." Brogan sniffed the air. "It's more than one. There are four. I believe it's them."

Four? If Story Teller came, that would make only three. They wouldn't be able to sense Hettie or Vas, because they'd be cloaked. But didn't Hettie say she'd cloak her parents for the trip as well? She couldn't remember. Ella let her mind wander out to see who was there through her senses.

"I can see them." Ella had her eyes closed to clearly see the image of who traveled so close. "Hettie and Vas are leading, and my parents follow. Oh, thank goodness! Story Teller is with them. Wait!" Ella opened her eyes and looked at Brogan. "Someone else is with them."

"Can you see who it is?" Brogan really didn't like surprises! Ella shook her head.

Chapter 47

"What do you mean, you can't see? You just told me you could see there was someone else." Brogan was annoyed. He hated unexpected situations, especially now, when he wasn't feeling in top shape. "Look again!"

"It'll do no good. Whoever's with them wears a very large cloak with the hood up; I can't see their face. I can't even tell you if it's male or female, or even if it's a fairy! We have to remember that whoever it is must be a friend. Otherwise they wouldn't be with Hettie and my parents."

Ella's words calmed Brogan, but he was still uneasy. Perhaps it was a Blue Wing who'd met up with them on their way here. That didn't feel right, though. It was someone they knew, but something just didn't feel right. Ella's voice interrupted his thoughts.

"Brogan, we should walk out to meet them." He could see the excitement in her eyes. This separation had been hard on her.

"They're still too far out. We'd need to walk too far from the village to meet them. I know you're excited, but we have to wait here for them. They may have been followed, and if you're out in the open, you'd make an easy target. I'm sorry, little one. They won't be long now."

The disappointment in Ella's eyes was difficult for Brogan to see. It hurt him that he'd upset her.

"I know you're right, but it's very difficult to wait when I know they're so close. If we have to wait, then can we wait on the outskirts of the village?"

"That we can do."

They walked to the outskirts. Brogan sat and waited, while Ella paced.

"It's taking them a long time to come such a short distance," Ella said on one of her many passes.

"Patience, little one. They'll be here soon." Brogan hoped, after all these years, that Hettie wasn't having a difficult time finding the village.

Half an hour passed, and there was still no sign of them. Ella was sure they should have already arrived. She allowed her mind to stretch out and see where they were. She could see them walking toward the village in a zig-zag fashion. They were very close now, but with the zig-zag path they followed, it was hard to judge how much time it would take them to get here. Ella explained the situation to Brogan.

"Hettie's making it difficult for anyone who might have followed. There may not even be anyone following, but Hettie won't take that chance. Could you see who the other traveler is?"

"No; they still have a cloak on, and the hood is pulled so far over I can't see." Ella's patience was wearing thin. They were so close, yet she couldn't go to them.

Another fifteen minutes passed, with Ella pacing. "Maybe I should contact Hettie and see if everything is okay. Maybe they're having problems of some kind. It shouldn't be taking them this long; they weren't that far away!"

"They'll be here any minute. You saw what Hettie was doing. Nothing's wrong; she's just covering their tracks."

"How can you be so calm, and how do you know there's nothing wrong? Maybe they're waiting for us to come and get them. Maybe someone's hurt."

"You're letting your imagination get the better of you. Did it look like someone was hurt? They're just covering their tracks. You need to give them more time."

"They should have been here by now!"

"What is all the yelling about?" Ella was surprised to hear another voice so close. When she turned around, she saw everyone walking toward them. It was her mother who'd spoken.

"Mother!" Ella picked up her dress and ran straight into her mother's arms.

"Oh, my baby, I was so worried." Ella's mother held her tightly. Both of them were crying.

"Would you have a hug for your father, or are you too old for that kind of thing now?" Ella turned and went into her father's arms. He wasn't crying, but his eyes were sure glistening.

"I'm so glad you're safe, my baby! Hettie told us what happened in the forest and before you left." As her father spoke, he hugged his daughter more tightly.

After Ella's father released her, she gave Story Teller a watery smile. "I was so worried you wouldn't come. If you only knew how glad I am you decided to make the journey." She gave Story Teller a big hug as well. When she stepped back, she saw that Story Teller was also crying.

Ella turned back to her parents and only then noticed the cloaked figure standing off to the side. In all the excitement, she'd forgotten someone else was with them. Ella looked to her mother for an answer, but her mother said nothing. She only grinned. Ella turned back to the cloaked figure and watched as small hands reached up to pull the hood back. It took a second to register who it was, but when she got over her shock, she ran toward her.

Chapter 48

"Astral! What are you doing here? It's so good to see you!" Astral was the last person Ella had expected to see under that hood. Ella and Astral hugged each other excitedly.

"I went to your parents' house every day, hoping you'd be home. When I went there this morning, Hettie and Vas were there, and everyone was getting ready to leave. I insisted that I come. I wanted to make sure you were all right, because you've never been away before, never mind for so long. I thought maybe something happened to you. You're almost like a sister to me, and we never go a day without talking. Your mother thought it would be good for you if I came, and my mother agreed I could go, so here I am." Ella laughed. Astral's rambling made things seem normal.

"I'm so glad you came. I missed you, too. Come—I'll show everyone around. It's a good thing I cleaned an extra house. You and I can stay in it."

"Oh, no, young fairy, you'll be staying with me and your father. Astral can stay with us. I need you close by this first night!" Ella could see that this separation had been difficult on her mother. She decided to let her mother have her way, but when she looked at Astral, she could tell she was disappointed. She would have to make sure they had time together, just the two of them.

Ella checked Brogan's reaction to Astral. When they made eye contact, he just raised his eyebrows. Ella knew he wasn't happy to see who the mystery guest was.

Everyone was walking into the village when Ella realized she hadn't thanked Hettie or Vas. As everyone followed Brogan, Ella walked up beside Hettie and stopped her. Vas was beside her, so he stopped, too. "Thank you both for bringing my family here. It may not seem like much, but it means the world to me. You have both done so much for me already." Ella looked at each of them, trying to find the right words.

"You don't need to thank me; I was glad to do it." Hettie kissed Ella's forehead. Ella gave Hettie a hug in return.

"Ella, I told your parents and Story Teller about your gifts. Your friend wasn't there when I did. Perhaps it would be better not to mention them to her for now. She does know about your ability to transport, however, because I told them about our magical attack." Hettie gave Ella a knowing look.

"I'm so glad you're safe, and don't worry, I won't say anything for now." Ella whispered these words to Hettie as she gave her another hug. Then she turned to Vas.

"Thank you, Vas, for everything. I'm glad to see you're safe." Ella bent down and gave Vas a hug. Vas's face turned scarlet. Even his little pointed ears were red. She winked and ran to catch up to the others.

Brogan led everyone on a quick tour of the village. Ella explained which tree huts she'd cleaned and showed her parents the one she'd picked out for them.

"My goodness, these tree huts are amazing! I wonder how they built these, because they look like the trees have grown them." Ella's mother couldn't stop looking at the tree hut she was going to live in.

Ella's father came to stand beside his wife. "This entire village is amazing. I've never seen anything like it."

Story Teller was also looking around in awe. "It's the most beautiful thing I've ever seen."

Ella smiled. Since she'd been here for a couple of days, she had forgotten the impact the village had when first seen. A sense of pride washed over her.

"Mother, I picked this tree hut for you because it's the one that most closely resembles your house at home. I believe it's just a little larger. The one beside it is the one closest to the ground. Father, I was hoping you'd build a ramp leading up to the door. It's the tree hut I've decided to live in. I want a ramp built so Brogan will be able to get up there at night." Ella could see the look on her mother's face as she spoke. She wasn't happy with this talk about living elsewhere; but the reality was that Ella was getting much too old to still be living with her parents. Ella took her mother's hand. "I'll be right beside you, but if it'll make you happy, I'll stay with you for the first few nights."

Her mother didn't say anything, but Ella knew her mother well. She would speak to Ella later when the others weren't around and try to guilt Ella into staying with her.

Hettie walked up beside Ella and quietly spoke to her. "There's no need for your father to build a ramp. Remember, you're able to speak to all living things. Simply ask the tree to grow something that Brogan can climb."

A look of wonder crossed Ella's face. "So the tree huts *were* grown! Wow." Ella looked at the tree hut she'd chosen for her parents. It seemed like such a wondrous thing, communicating with the trees. The fact that she could do this, too, took her breath away! Ella looked back to Hettie, who was watching her reaction. When their eyes met, Hettie smiled.

Brogan got everyone's attention again and continued the tour. He showed them the river and the clothes-drying line. Ella had forgotten she still had bedding hung there.

"Looks like someone was busy." Ella's mother seemed surprised.

"These weren't quite dry earlier. I'll have to come and get them later."

"Don't worry, Ella. Your father and I can collect them later. It'll give us something to do."

Everyone continued on in the direction of the village bower. Ella had made sure to clean up before everyone arrived. Brogan said he was feeling much better and no longer needed to stay inside. As they entered the bower, Story Teller turned to Ella with shock and surprise in her eyes.

"What's wrong, Story Teller? Don't you like this bower? I know it's a little different, and it might be a little smaller than your last one, but I'm sure in time we can add on. This bower even has lodgings built onto the back. Or perhaps I should say, grown onto the back." Ella was concerned that if Story Teller didn't like it here, she'd want to go back.

"Oh, no, little one, this is a beautiful bower. I'm sure I'll be very happy here. I was just a little shocked that you were able to get a fire started in the pit. Normally, in a communal bower like this, only a keeper of the fire would be able to start the fire."

"I didn't start it. It started on its own shortly after Brogan and I came in." Ella looked to Brogan for confirmation.

"It's true. We were almost to the pit when it started on its own. It made quite the noise before it started," Brogan said.

"That's how you start a communal fire. Only the presence of a keeper is needed to start, or, in this case, restart, the fire. It would seem you have the fire element within. This would make sense, considering what happened at your fire ceremony. You could be a keeper of the fire, Ella. Perhaps we should start some of the training required."

"I could be a keeper of the fire, but I know it's not my path. Fire is one of the elements I control, but my destiny isn't to be the keeper of it. I'll leave that to you. I'm sure there will come a time when the right fairy makes him- or herself known. When that time comes, it'll be him or her whom you train."

Ella knew these words were true. She smiled. "So you really do like the bower? Would you like to see the lodgings? If you don't like it, you can pick out a tree hut instead."

"I'm sure the lodgings will be more than fine. And yes, I love the bower. I know I'll be very happy here. How convenient to have the lodgings right behind the bower. Someone was thinking!" Story Teller's last words were said more to herself. She followed Ella to see her new home.

Chapter 49

Everyone stayed in the village bower to eat their evening meal, for Brogan's sake. Brogan had gone on a hunt shortly after everyone arrived and brought back enough for himself plus enough to make a meal for everyone else the next day. Ella's mother had brought a large basket, which was crammed full of food, for everyone's meal that night. Even after everyone had eaten, there was still enough food to feed them for two more meals. Hettie said she'd make the next evening's meal from the meat Brogan had brought them.

They sat around the outdoor fire afterward, enjoying the calm evening. Ella decided to tell all of them—including Astral—about her encounter with the Creator; she felt Astral had a right to know about her, too. She told them how she was unable to help Brogan and how the Creator had saved him. Then she told them what the Creator had told her. She decided to leave out the gift of energy. That was something she didn't want to share with Astral there. She didn't know why, but she felt sure this was the right decision. As she told the story, she could see that Astral looked very uncomfortable. It was the first time Ella had seen Astral speechless. Her parents asked many questions, which she answered. Story Teller said nothing, but she looked rather pleased.

Hettie smiled. "I'm glad I told you of her before she came to you, although I wasn't sure you believed me."

"I wasn't sure I did believe you, even though I knew you believed it yourself. All I can say is, I definitely believe now!"

"Well, if you hadn't told her about the Creator, she wouldn't have prayed to her for help. So really we should also be thanking you for helping to save Brogan's life." Ella's father spoke the words a little more quietly than usual. Ella knew it frightened her parents to think of how close they'd come to losing both her and Brogan.

It was getting late, and everyone decided to go to their designated houses. Vas wasn't comfortable sleeping inside the village and went to find himself a place to sleep.

"Why isn't he staying here with us?" Ella asked Hettie. She already knew the answer.

"He's not comfortable with everyone around. He never has been comfortable in a crowd. Don't worry; he'll often go off on his own, but he'll come back to the village in the morning. Goodnight, Ella. Enjoy your time with your family." Hettie gave Ella a quick hug and walked toward her tree hut. Using her pole and her magic, she floated up to the veranda and went inside.

Ella looked at Astral and laughed. "I thought we'd have to make a ladder or steps of some kind for her. Sometimes I forget she's a powerful witch." Astral laughed with her.

Astral, Ella, and Ella's parents flew up to their tree hut. Even though Ella's father offered to fly him up, Brogan decided to stay outside, below their tree. He'd already made a small bed for himself.

Once inside, Ella and Astral went upstairs and made a pallet of blankets on the floor for Astral to sleep in. They would stay in the same room.

"This feels like when we were smaller and we'd have sleepovers at each other's houses. Do you remember those, Ella?" Astral pulled down the blanket and got ready to climb into bed.

"I remember them well. We'd always stay up and talk almost all night. Our parents would get so angry at us! Your younger sisters would be so jealous when you'd come over to my house." Ella got into bed and put a pillow behind her so she could sit up and talk.

"They were always jealous about something. They were even upset I was coming here with your parents. They thought they should be able to come, too." Astral was laughing.

The two of them talked for several hours. They spoke of normal everyday things, and Astral told Ella all about her love life. It was nice to pretend for a while that everything was normal. Ella would have to return to reality tomorrow, but, for right now, all was good. After talking for a while longer, the girls agreed it'd been a long day and decided to go to sleep.

Ella was just about to fall asleep when she heard Astral's question. "You're never coming back, are you?"

She knew exactly what Astral meant. "No. This is my home now. I must stay here."

"Things have changed so much. Sometimes I wish we could go back to when we were young and everything was simple."

Ella heard the sadness in her friend's voice. "You'll always be welcome here, Astral. You could even move here if you wanted."

"Thanks, Ella. Ella?"

"Yes?"

"I'm sorry."

"Sorry? For what?" Ella was surprised.

"Well, for everything."

Ella wasn't sure what Astral meant, but she was too tired to pursue it now. She'd have to remember to ask Astral about it later. It bothered her to hear such sadness in her friend's voice.

Ella had been fast asleep when something woke her. She sat up in bed and looked around the room. When she turned to the side Astral was sleeping on, she found her friend standing over her.

"Astral? What's wrong?"

"Nothing; I just needed to go to the bathroom. Sorry for waking you. Go back to sleep."

Ella watched Astral get back into bed and turned around to go back to sleep.

Chapter 50

When Ella woke up, Astral was still sleeping soundly. Knowing Astral hadn't had a good night, she decided to let her friend sleep a little longer. She went downstairs and found her mother and father sitting at the kitchen table.

Ella hugged them both. "Good morning. How did you sleep?" She couldn't help noticing how tired her mother looked.

"Your father slept like the dead. I had a little more trouble getting to sleep in a strange bed. Where's Astral?"

"She didn't have a good night, either. She was still sleeping when I got up, so I let her be. She'll get up when she's ready."

"She probably isn't used to sleeping in a strange place, either. I don't think she's ever left the village before, so I was more than a little surprised that she was so insistent on coming with us. I didn't think the two of you were that close anymore. Perhaps your leaving made her realize how much your friendship meant to her."

"You know what I thought was strange?" Ella's father looked first to his wife and then to his daughter. "I thought it was strange that Brogan took the fact that Astral was with us so well. I know he doesn't like her much. That must have been some knock on the head he got."

"There isn't much he could say. She was already here. I know he's not happy about it, but, for my sake, he won't say much. Just so you know, it was more than just a knock. He almost died in my arms. I thank the Creator for his life."

Ella paused and looked at her parents. She lowered her voice. "There's something else you should know about my visit from the Creator." She told her parents of the gift the Creator had given her. "Never again will I worry about not having enough energy to help someone. It was the worst feeling in the world to think he would die because I didn't have the power to save him." Tears rolled down her face again. Goodness, what was wrong with her? She was becoming such a crybaby! "Anyway, I'd rather talk of something else." Ella wiped her cheeks with her dress sleeve. Her mother gave her a hug and then ushered her to the table, where a plate of nuts, fruit, and cheese awaited her.

"How was your journey yesterday? I never really had time to ask you. What do you think of Hettie?" Ella picked at the food.

"I think she's a lovely person and rather likable. Anyone who would go out of their way to help my baby girl can't be bad." Ella's father spoke carefully.

"Mother? What do you think of her?"

"I guess she's all right."

"What do you mean, you guess? Did something happen yesterday? Did Hettie say or do something to upset you?" Ella looked from her mother to her father.

"No, of course not. She seems quite lovely, but I'm a little surprised at how close the two of you are. You really should be more careful, Ella. We know very little about her," her mother said, playing with a loose thread on her dress.

Ella couldn't believe what she was hearing. "Hettie is kind, generous, and doesn't pretend to be something she's not. You wouldn't happen to be jealous of her?"

"Of course I'm not jealous! It's just that out of the blue she sends a message to have you go to her, and now that you've spent a few days with her, you two are suddenly very close. It makes me wonder what's in it for her."

"She isn't gaining anything from this! If anything, she's losing. She lost her home because of me, and she gave up her life to come and help me." Ella took a deep breath. "Besides, I'm also close to Story Teller, and you don't have a problem with her. What's the difference?"

"Story Teller is different. She's almost like family, and she's a fairy! Hettie's a witch!" Her mother's voice had gone up in volume.

There was a stunned silence. Ella couldn't believe what her mother had said. Even her father looked surprised. Ella kept her voice down with effort. "Mother, I'm truly surprised at you. All my life I've looked up to you, admired you, and wanted to be like you. Until this very moment, I've never been disappointed in you. The reason I'm here is that people from our village want to kill me! They wish me harm because my wings are blue, not silver—basically, because I'm not like them! You dislike Hettie because she's different and hasn't any wings like we do. What makes you different from the people who dislike me?"

Ella waited while her words sunk in. Her mother looked stunned. Ella added, "If you ever gave Hettie the chance, you'd find that you and she are quite alike. I thought the two of you would be good friends, but I guess I was wrong. Because she has no wings and she's a witch, you'd rather shun her."

Ella walked toward the door. Never in her life had she spoken to her mother like that. To do so now made her tummy turn. She felt like she might be sick! She couldn't believe her mother would say something like that. Her mother was damning someone because they were different, even after all Ella had been through because other fairies were doing the same thing to her. It hurt deeply.

She'd just stepped onto the veranda when her father caught up to her. "Ella, don't you think you were a little hard on your mother?"

"No! No, I don't. What she just said makes her no different from the fairies who want to hurt me. I cannot and will not have that kind of attitude within this village. It goes against everything I believe in and stand for. There'll be all sorts of magical beings coming to this village, and I will not turn them away because they are different. Also, I will not allow them to be shunned or mistreated because of those differences."

Ella could no longer look her father in the eye. "I can make no exceptions, not even for my own mother. How would it look?"

Ella didn't wait to hear her father's response. She flew down to Brogan and started walking in the direction of the river. Once they got there, Ella sat on the bank and watched the water rush over the rocks.

"I overheard your conversation with your mother. You might not know this, but I have exceptional hearing," Brogan said, sitting down beside her.

"I just feel sick, Brogan. How can she say things like that and yet be so angry with those who hurt me because my wings are blue? It's hypocritical of her, don't you think?"

"Ella, you have to understand that change is difficult for everyone. All of this will take time for your mother to get used to. Plus, I think you're right about her being jealous of Hettie. Give her time. You'll see that things will work themselves out. Your mother will come around."

"Well, she better, because I don't want that kind of attitude around me or anyone else in this village. This village is going to be a safe haven for all creatures. It doesn't matter who they are!"

"I'm very proud of you, little one!"

"Why would you be proud of me?" Ella looked carefully at Brogan. Maybe that hit to the head *had* done something to him.

"I'm proud of you for standing up for what you believe in, even though it meant standing up to your own parents. You handled that situation very well, and you didn't once raise your voice.

You've grown much over these last few days." Brogan leaned his upper body toward Ella and nudged her playfully. "Little one!"

Ella tried not to smile, but she couldn't help herself. She nudged him back.

Chapter 51

Ella and Brogan sat by the river for a while. After some time, Brogan finally spoke. "We should get back. Astral will probably be awake by now, wondering what happened to you."

As Brogan had predicted, Astral was waiting for Ella when they got back. Ella's parents weren't there, and she felt ashamed at her relief over not having to face her parents so soon.

Ella smiled at her friend. "Good morning, sleepyhead. I let you sleep in because you didn't seem to have a very good night." Ella sat down at the table.

"Thanks for that. I didn't sleep well at all. By the way, your parents were here when I came down, and your mother was crying. Your father took her out for a walk. I have to say, you don't look very happy, either."

"My mother and I had an argument." Ella still felt sick over it.

"I'm shocked! I didn't think you and your mother ever argued! You know how my mother and I argue. I was always a little jealous of you and your mother's relationship."

Ella looked at Astral in surprise. "Really? That sounds so strange." Ella paused, "This is the first I've argued with my mother, and it doesn't feel very good!"

"Yeah, I know how you feel." Astral smiled. "The worst for me was when my mother would say, 'Why can't you be more like Ella?' She'd always say that after we had a disagreement."

"I'm willing to bet she hasn't said that since my wings turned blue."

Astral gave Ella a sheepish grin. "No, I guess she hasn't. So much has changed since your wings turned blue." Astral walked to the door and looked outside. "Ella, I want to tell you that I'm sorry for how things worked out. When your wings turned blue, well, it changed things for everyone."

Ella joined Astral at the door. They looked out over the forest.

"I guess you could say it was a bit of a shock for everyone," Ella said. "However, if I could go back and stop it from happening, I don't think I would. It happened for a reason. I'm not sure what that reason is, but I know there is one." Ella smiled at the shocked, disbelieving look on her friend's face. Ella knew Astral wouldn't understand.

Astral put her hands into her dress pockets. "I'd think you'd want to change it if you could. Look what's happened since your wings turned blue. You want to be different, to have all this happening?"

Ella walked over to the fireplace, which had no fire. "I don't want to be different, Astral. I just want to be me. If having blue wings is what makes me who I am, then how could I want to change that?"

"You know, there are many Silver Wings who feel you're an abomination that shouldn't exist. They worry about your powers. Some believe you'll lash out at them for the past. They fear you, Ella."

Ella looked at the floor. It hurt her greatly to hear her best friend say these words. "I do know this. Apparently there are some from our village who feel this way. They've been plotting against me and wish me dead. That's why I came here."

Ella heard Astral come up behind her. Astral spoke quietly. "I'm glad you know. Perhaps then you'll understand what I must do. It'll make it easier now."

Ella turned around and found Astral standing directly in front of her. In Astral's hand was a large bejeweled knife that was serrated on one side and smooth but sharp on the other. Ella was in complete and total shock.

"I'm sorry, Ella!" Astral said in a barely audible whisper. Tears streamed down her face. Ella watched as Astral's arm flew up and then swooped back down, aiming the knife at her heart. Ella's shock had left her immobile. She heard Brogan screaming from below, but she couldn't speak or move.

As she watched the knife come closer, she heard another loud scream and saw, from the corner of her eye, a small shape sail through the air. One second the knife was there, the next it was gone. Through Ella's shocked fog, she saw Vas crash in and tackle Astral, sending them both to the floor. At first it was difficult to see who was who because there was such a blur of tangled arms and legs. All movement suddenly stopped, and Ella saw Astral leaning over Vas, ready to plunge the knife into him.

The veil of shock lifted, and Ella raised both her hands, yelling as loud as she could, "*Stop!*"

Everything around her instantly froze. Astral's knife was only inches from piercing Vas's throat.

Holy fairy farts! Astral had just tried to kill her! Ella slowly walked toward the two frozen figures. Moving through stopped time was like moving through thick mud. All of her movements were slow and difficult. When she finally reached Astral and Vas, she bent down and grabbed Vas by his tunic. Using all her strength, Ella pulled Vas out from under Astral and her deadly knife. She wasn't able to pull him far, but it wouldn't matter as long as she pulled him far enough so that when the knife continued its journey down, no part of him would be under it.

Just pulling Vas that short distance made her extremely short of breath. Even the air seemed different when time was stopped.

She took a second to catch her breath and then put both her hands in front of her again. Quietly she said, "Begin!"

Everything sprang back to life. Astral's knife crashed down, lodging itself into the kitchen floor. Rage crossed her face.

"What have you done?" Astral screamed. With her face turning an alarming red, she looked crazy. Astral pulled on the knife until she freed it from the floor. The sudden release of the knife sent Astral flying backward a few steps. With some quick footwork, however, she regained her balance and lunged at Ella with the knife high above her head.

This time Ella was prepared. She quickly stepped over an unconscious Vas, raising her hand as she moved. A large burst of energy hit its target, sending Astral flying across the kitchen and into the back wall. Astral hit the wall, slid down, and landed on the floor in a slump.

There was a second of total silence before Vas began to stir. Ella heard the kitchen door open and others come in. With everything going on around her, she could only stand there and stare in horror. What had she done?

At some point during the commotion, the knife had managed to bury itself deep into Astral's chest. Astral was still breathing, but Ella was sure the knife wound, without intervention, would be fatal. As she stared at the knife, she heard her name. Astral was calling her.

Chapter 52

Ella walked toward Astral. Someone told her to stay back, she wasn't sure who it was; and, frankly, she didn't care. Without looking, she motioned them away. Once she reached Astral, she bent down and took her friend's hand. She could feel Astral's life energy rapidly running out.

"Why, Astral? Why would you do it?" Ella's voice trembled at the betrayal.

"My mother's grandfather was named Jeddah. After he helped destroy the Blue Wings, he was banished from his village. My family believed he did the right thing and was unfairly banished. Since then, my family has watched and waited to see if the prophecy of the Blue Wings would come true. If it did, they would take care of this blue-winged fairy before anyone else was hurt. Imagine my mother's surprise when the prophecy did come true and the fairy turned out to be her daughter's best friend." Astral laughed weakly.

"When your wings turned blue, she told me it would be up to me to take care of you. If I didn't, she would banish me from the family and run me out of the village." Astral looked up at Ella and took several deep breaths. "Last night, when you woke up, I had the knife in my hand, but I couldn't do it. I couldn't kill you. When you had the fight with your mother this morning, I thought at last you might understand! I decided to go through with it because I wanted to be able to go home and have my mother look at me as your mother looks at you. I wanted her to finally be proud of me, and I wanted her love." Astral gave a weak, choking laugh that turned into a rasping cough.

"It was you who threw the rock at me?" Ella felt numb.

"My mother was with me. I had no choice. She was the one who screamed out the warnings. I'm so sorry, Ella! I'm really, really sorry!"

Ella laid her hand on Astral's wound. "Let me help you, Astral, and when you're better, you can stay here with me. You'll be safe here!" Ella prepared to heal her friend, but, before she could start, Astral weakly pushed her hand away.

"Ella, please, no. Just leave me be." Ella looked at her pleadingly. "It's all right, Ella. You know I couldn't stay here. My mother would hurt me through my siblings, my sisters and my brother. You don't understand her madness. It's so bad now that even my father has left. It'll be better this way, for everyone. Allow me to have a hero's death, at least in my mother's eyes."

"I had no idea how bad things were or how sick your mother is. I'm so sorry for you and all you've gone through." Ella laid her hand on Astral's.

"You actually forgive me?"

Ella was crying. "Of course I forgive you. I love you."

Astral's breath became more labored. With her eyes closed, Astral spoke her last words. "I'm so sorry, Ella. I love you, too."

Ella held Astral and watched as she took her last few breaths. Ella stayed in the same position for several minutes after Astral died. When she finally looked up, she saw her family and extended family standing quietly behind her. Her mother helped her to stand. She tried to give Ella a hug, but Ella pulled away and walked to the door.

Just before she walked out, she said, "I think I need some air."

She flew back to the river and sat on a large branch that hung high over the water. There she sat, leaning against the trunk of a tree, allowing the leaves from the branch above to hang down and partially cover her.

She tried to watch the river quietly flow past, but she couldn't see much through her tears as they poured silently down her cheeks.

Chapter 53

She knew Brogan had followed her and was waiting below her. He didn't say a word; he just sat quietly, allowing her time to grieve. After her tears petered out, she flew down to sit at the edge of the river. Brogan joined her, and she rested her head on his neck. They sat like that for quite a while before Ella straightened up again.

"I suppose you want to tell me 'I told you so'? You said you didn't like her or trust her."

"She was a pawn. Her mother's sickness was forced onto her. It's a sad thing to see."

"What will happen to her?"

"Hettie has used her magic to send Astral and a note back to her family. The note explains what happened and points out that a young fairy needlessly died today."

Ella hung her head. "It's a betrayal of the worst kind. She was like a sister to me! I don't understand."

"It's better if you don't. To understand would make you as sick as them. We must accept it and move on."

Ella stood and stepped to the water's edge. With a flick of her hand, the water parted, leaving a small space free of water as the rest of the river traveled around it.

"Vas saved my life today. I totally froze when I saw her standing there with that knife. If Vas hadn't come in when he did, I wouldn't be here right now."

"You froze because you were in shock! Astral was the last person you thought would do something like that. It's understandable."

"Nothing about this is understandable!" Ella whispered.

"That's impressive, what you can do with water. You have the element of water as well as fire. It's unusual for a fairy to have control over more than one element."

Ella looked at Brogan. "That's me, unusual," she said sarcastically. "I believe it was said I would control all the elements." Ella curled her hands into fists. "Oh, how I am blessed!" Her voice was quiet and laced with self-loathing. She turned away.

Brogan stood at Ella's side. "You should know your mother went to Hettie and told her about the argument you had. She also apologized to Hettie."

"I'm proud of my mother. I know they'll become good friends; they have a lot in common."

"Ella, look at me." Ella grudgingly turned to look at Brogan. "What happened today was beyond terrible, but I can guarantee you'll have other days that'll be just as bad or even worse! There's a war going on that we never agreed to fight in, and we have no control over what others might do. What happened today wasn't our doing, and Astral's death wasn't your fault!"

Ella looked back at the river.

"You can't dwell on this, little one; it will make you crazy. You need to look at the bigger picture and think of everyone who is depending on you. Others like you will be coming soon, and they will look to you for guidance! Remember, they didn't ask to have this happen to them, either, and you can be sure they've all gone through their own traumas."

Brogan waited for a moment. "The white streak in your hair, was it from stopping time?"

Ella pulled her hair in front of her face. A small white streak was indeed running down the front. "It must be; it wasn't there before!" She let her hair fall back.

They watched the river for a while. Ella turned her face to the sun; she'd never felt so cold in all her life. While she was trying to let the sun warm her, a strange sensation started coursing through her. She let her mind wander out.

"Brogan, a Blue Wing is coming, and he's fairly close. He's calling to me. I can feel him in my blood, and I know he's very powerful. It won't take him long to get here."

"How long before he arrives?"

"He's about a week away, maybe less."

"And so it begins." Brogan smiled.

"I'm not sure I'm ready for this!"

"You're ready, little one."

"I'm glad one of us thinks so." Ella paused. "There's something else I need to talk to you about before we go back."

"All right." Brogan's tone was hesitant.

"I had a dream last night." Ella looked Brogan in the eye. "I don't think you'll like it much."

Chapter 54

Brogan exhaled and rolled his eyes. He waited for Ella to tell him about the dream, but she said nothing.

"Well? You better tell me what the dream was about."

"I don't really want to, because if I tell you, then it becomes real, and I'll actually have to do something about it."

"Ella, spill it!"

"I'm not even sure who was speaking to me in the dream; I never saw them, and their voice was only a light whisper. My guess is it was either the Creator or Eamon. Anyway, I was told several things. First, I must go to the elves, gnomes, and goblins to try to reestablish ties with them."

"That would make sense, and it's something I was going to suggest to you later," Brogan said.

"I was also told that, more importantly, I needed to find the brownies and make contact with them. The only problem is, I've never heard of brownies. Have you?"

"Interesting! I've heard of them, but only in a folktale. I didn't think they were real." Brogan paused. "We'll have to ask Hettie."

"Okay, but not right away. I want to wait until most of the Blue Wings arrive before we speak about this dream to anyone else. I'm not sure why, but I have a feeling now isn't the time."

Brogan nodded in agreement.

"I was told one more thing in my dream: I must find the Book of the Dead. It was last seen when it was used to destroy the Blue Wings all those years ago. It's the fairies' most powerful book, and others want to use it against me. We need to find it before they do."

"What do we do with it if we find it?"

"I don't know."

"Where do we look for it?"

"Brogan, I don't know! I don't have the answers; I'm just telling you what I was told in the dream."

"There's no reason to be upset. The answers will come when you're ready. All in good time." Brogan waited for Ella to take a few breaths.

"You're right. I'm still upset about Astral. Brogan, please make sure you don't mention my dream to anyone until I say so. My parents don't need the extra worry, and I'm not ready to deal with anyone's opinions on the matter."

"I've already agreed, little one. Mum's the word." Brogan shrugged. "Is there anything else about your dream I should know?"

"Isn't that enough?" Ella raised her eyebrows.

Brogan grunted. "I would say that's enough. Although from your tone, I expected far worse."

He brushed against Ella's leg. "I guess we should go tell the others that we can expect the first Blue Wing very soon. Hettie will be very excited to hear this."

"I guess we should. Before we go, I want to say something." Ella wrapped her arms around Brogan's neck. "Thank you," Ella whispered into his ear.

Brogan stepped back. "'Thank you'? Why are you thanking me?"

"Well, for being here when I needed you most, and for understanding."

Brogan tilted his head. "Isn't that what being family is all about? Being there for each other?"

Ella was shocked. Those were words she'd never dreamed she'd hear from Brogan, and they brought tears to her eyes. She dropped her head, wiped her tears, and then very quietly said, "Yes, I suppose that's exactly what family does for each other."

Brogan smiled from ear to ear. "Come, little one; let's go tell everyone of our impending visitor."

Ella could only nod.

They headed back silently, side by side. They hadn't gone far when Brogan stepped in closer, nosing Ella's hand up onto his neck. She looked down at her hand and then at Brogan, and she smiled. It was nice to finally be home with her true family.

Dawn Williscroft is a passionate reader and writer. Her two sons are her main inspiration, and she currently lives in High Prairie, Alberta, Canada.